GCSE OCR Gateway Biology Higher Workbook

This book is for anyone doing **GCSE OCR Gateway Biology** at higher level.

It's full of **tricky questions**... each one designed to make you **sweat** — because that's the only way you'll get any **better**.

There are questions to see **what facts** you know. There are questions to see how well you can **apply those facts**. And there are questions to see what you know about **how science works**.

It's also got some daft bits in to try and make the whole experience at least vaguely entertaining for you.

What CGP is all about

Our sole aim here at CGP is to produce the highest quality books — carefully written, immaculately presented and dangerously close to being funny.

Then we work our socks off to get them out to you — at the cheapest possible prices.

Contents

Module B1 — Understanding Ourselves

Module B2 — Understanding Our Environment

Module B3 — Living and Growing

Module B4 — It's a Green World

Module B5 — The Living Body

Module B6 — Beyond the Microscope

Published by CGP

Editors:
Luke Antieul, Joe Brazier, Emma Elder, Murray Hamilton, Edmund Robinson, Hayley Thompson.

Contributors:
Jane Davies, James Foster, Derek Harvey, Rebecca Harvey, Dr Iona MJ Hamilton,
Philip Rushworth, Claire Ruthven, Adrian Schmit.

ISBN: 978 1 84762 610 3

Data used to draw graph on page 63 developed by the National Center for Health Statistics in collaboration with the National Center for Chronic Disease Prevention and Health Promotion (2000). http://www.cdc.gov/growthcharts

Every effort has been made to locate copyright holders and obtain permission to reproduce sources. For those sources where it has been difficult to trace the originator of the work, we would be grateful for information. If any copyright holder would like us to make an amendment to the acknowledgements, please notify us and we will gladly update the book at the next reprint. Thank you.

With thanks to Helen Brace, Janet Cruse-Sawyer, Mary Faulkner, Ben Fletcher, Julie Jackson, and Karen Wells for the proofreading.

With thanks to Laura Jakubowski for the copyright research.

Printed by Elanders Ltd, Newcastle upon Tyne.
Clipart from Corel®

Based on the classic CGP style created by Richard Parsons.

Fitness and Blood Pressure

Q1 Fill in the blanks in the paragraph, choosing the correct words from the list below.

oxygen lower higher mmAu diastolic
systolic mmHg nitrogen fitness health Germany

When a doctor measures your blood pressure, two readings are taken.

The .... pressure is the pressure when your heart contracts.

It is the .... reading for your blood pressure. The other

reading is taken when your heart relaxes. This is the ....

pressure and is the .... reading. Blood pressure is

measured in ....

Q2 **Low blood pressure** can cause health problems. Give **two** health problems that people with low blood pressure might have.

....

....

Q3 The table shows some information on the **lifestyles** of Tricia and Dave.

Name	Occupation	Cigarettes smoked per day	Units of alcohol consumed per week
Tricia	Retired	0	4
Dave	Stock broker	40	28

a) How many more units of alcohol does Dave consume each week compared to Tricia?

....

b) Who do you think is more likely to have **high blood pressure**, Tricia or Dave?
Give **one** reason for your answer.

....

....

c) State **one** health problem that can result from **high blood pressure**.

....

Fitness and Blood Pressure

Q4 Petunia says: "**Fitness** means the same thing as being **healthy**."
Is Petunia right? Explain your answer.

....

....

....

Q5 **Stamina** is a good indicator of fitness and cardiovascular efficiency.

a) Which of the following is a way of measuring stamina? Circle the correct answer.

A — Measuring oxygen uptake during exercise

B — Measuring the fastest speed you can run

C — Measuring your lung capacity

D — Calculating your Body Mass Index (BMI)

b) What is cardiovascular efficiency?

....

c) Apart from stamina and cardiovascular efficiency, give three things that could be measured to assess fitness.

1. .... 2. .... 3. ....

Q6 Jack has **high blood pressure**. He is overweight, eats very few fruits and vegetables and relies mostly on ready meals and take-aways. He does no regular exercise. He does drink alcohol, but only about three pints of beer in a week.

Suggest two ways in which Jack might reduce his blood pressure without taking drugs.

1. ....

2. ....

Top Tips: Don't forget that factors like smoking, being overweight, alcohol and stress only increase the **chances** of someone developing high blood pressure. They're not guaranteed to cause it.

High Blood Pressure and Heart Disease

Q1 Fill in the blanks in the paragraph, choosing the correct words from the list below.

restricting	stroke	increasing	oxygen	plug
plaques	nitrogen	heart attack	thrombosis	tartar

The coronary arteries supply the heart muscle with blood. The formation of .... in the walls of the coronary arteries can cause the arteries to narrow, ... blood flow. A narrow coronary artery can be completely blocked by a .... If this happens, part of the heart muscle will be cut off from its .... supply — causing a ....

Q2 **Cholesterol** is a fatty substance needed in the body.

a) Complete the following sentence.

A diet high in .... has been linked to high levels of cholesterol in the blood.

b) Describe what might happen if too much cholesterol builds up in your arteries.

....

....

Q3 People are often encouraged to reduce the amount of **salt** that they consume in their diet.

Explain how a diet that is **high in salt** can increase the risk of a heart attack.

....

....

Q4 Amy smokes cigarettes regularly. She has **high blood pressure** and her doctor thinks that her smoking is causing it. **Nicotine** and **carbon monoxide** are both found in cigarette smoke. Explain how each of these chemicals can increase blood pressure.

Nicotine: ....

....

Carbon monoxide: ....

....

....

Eating Healthily

Q1 Draw lines to join each **nutrient** with what it is made from.

Carbohydrate	Amino acids
Protein	Glycerol
Fat	Simple sugars
	Fatty acids

Q2 Complete the table to show how some nutrients are **stored** in the body.

Nutrient	Storage in the body
	Stored in the liver as glycogen or converted to fats
	Not stored in the body
Fat	

Q3 All **essential amino acids** can be found in **first class proteins**.

a) What are essential amino acids?

....

b) What are first class proteins?

....

Q4 Wendy and June both work as IT technicians. Wendy is training to run a marathon and goes to the gym every evening. June doesn't enjoy sport and prefers playing chess in her spare time. Who needs more **protein** and **carbohydrate** in their diet — June or Wendy? Explain your answer.

....

....

....

Q5 Some people do not include certain foods in their diet for religious, personal or medical reasons.

a) Give one **medical reason** why people might avoid certain foods.

....

b) Suggest one **personal reason** why someone might choose to be a vegetarian.

....

Diet Problems

Q1 **Kwashiorkor** is a condition caused by lack of protein in the diet.

a) Give **two** reasons why this condition is most common in developing countries.

....

....

....

b) Calculate the EAR of protein for a 75 kg man.

....

c) Explain why the EAR of protein varies with:

i) age.

....

ii) pregnancy.

....

Q2 **Anorexia nervosa** and **bulimia nervosa** are psychological disorders that cause **under-nutrition**.

a) State **two** possible causes of these disorders.

....

b) Give **three** health problems that a poor diet resulting from these disorders may cause.

....

Q3 **Body mass index (BMI)** is calculated to help determine a person's ideal weight.

a) Daniel is 1.7 m tall and weighs 76 kg. Calculate his BMI.

....

$$\text{BMI} = \frac{\text{body mass in kg}}{(\text{height in m})^2}$$

b) Look at the table on the right.
What is Daniel's weight description?

....

Body Mass Index	Weight Description
below 18.5	underweight
18.5 - 24.9	normal
25 - 29.9	overweight
30 - 40	moderately obese
above 40	severely obese

Infectious Disease

Q1 a) Circle the correct words to complete the sentences below.

> Malaria is a disease caused by a microorganism called a **virus / protozoan**. The microorganism is a **parasite / guest** and the animal it infects is called a **host / agent**. The infection is transmitted from person to person by mosquitoes. An organism which transfers a disease without actually getting it is called a **vector / insect**. Mosquitoes feed on **blood / snot**. When they bite an **old / infected** animal they take in the malarial microorganism and then pass it on to the next animal they bite.

b) **i)** We know that **mosquitoes** spread malaria when they **bite people**.
Suggest **one** way that we can use this knowledge to reduce the spread of infection.

....

....

ii) We also know that mosquitoes breed in **areas of water**.
Suggest **one** way that we can use this knowledge to reduce the spread of infection.

....

Q2 John catches a **cold**. A cold is an infectious disease.

a) How do pathogens cause the symptoms of an infectious disease?

....

....

b) How do John's white blood cells recognise the cold-causing pathogen?

....

....

c) Shortly after recovering, John is infected with a cold-causing pathogen that he hasn't had before. Will he get ill? Explain your answer.

....

....

Preventing and Treating Infectious Disease

Q1 **Immunisation** involves injecting dead or inactive microorganisms into the body.

a) Tick the box to show whether the following statements about polio immunisation are **true** or **false**.

	True	False
i) The dead or inactive polio microorganisms have some of the same antigens as the live pathogen.	☐	☐
ii) White blood cells produce antibodies against the antigens on the injected polio microorganisms.	☐	☐
iii) After immunisation, memory cells can produce antibodies to fight infections of typhoid.	☐	☐
iv) Immunisation is a type of passive immunity.	☐	☐

b) Circle the correct words to complete the paragraph.

In active immunity the immune system makes its own **antibodies / antigens**, but in passive immunity they come from **vaccination / another organism**. Active immunity is **permanent / temporary**, but passive immunity is **permanent / temporary**.

Q2 a) Give two **benefits** of immunisation.

1. ....

2. ....

b) Give **one** possible **risk** of immunisation.

....

Q3 John gets injected with the **rubella vaccine** but James doesn't. Soon afterwards both boys are exposed to the rubella virus. Explain in detail why James gets ill but John doesn't.

....

....

....

....

....

Preventing and Treating Infectious Disease

Q4 Tick the box to show whether the following statements are **true** or **false**.

	True	False
a) Antibiotics help bacteria to grow.	☐	☐
b) MRSA is an example of an antibiotic-resistant strain of bacteria.	☐	☐
c) Doctors overprescribing antibiotics has helped antibiotic-resistant bacteria to develop.	☐	☐

Q5 Rachel has a **viral infection**, but when she visits her doctor he refuses to give her antibiotics.

a) Explain why her doctor is right.

....

....

b) What type of drug could her doctor prescribe?

....

Q6 The graph shows the number of **bacteria Y** in Gary's blood during a two-week course of **antibiotics**.

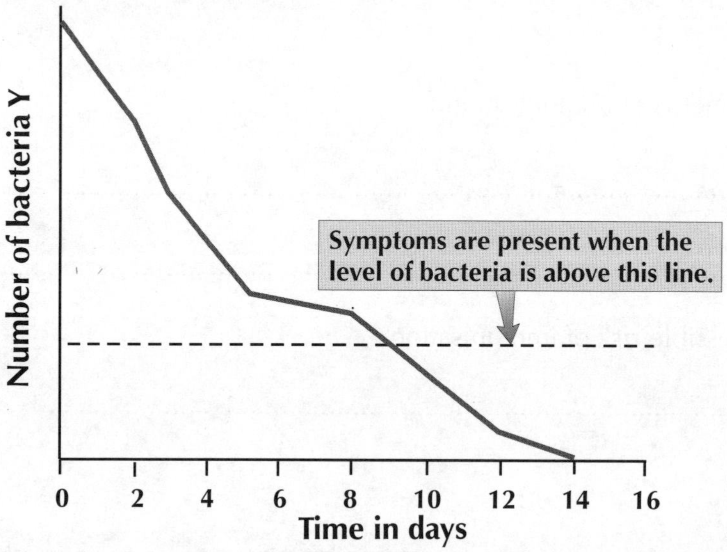

a) How long after starting the course of antibiotics will Gary's symptoms disappear?

....

b) Why is it important for Gary to **finish** his full course of antibiotics?

....

....

Top Tips: Nobody really thought about all the problems that the misuse of antibiotics might cause until it was too late. Now we've got to come up with new ways to fight these antibiotic-resistant 'superbugs' — my suggestion of a microscopic rolled-up newspaper wasn't met with much approval.

Cancer and Drug Development

Q1 **Cancer** is caused by cells dividing out of control.

a) Explain the difference between **benign** and **malignant** cancer tumours.

....

....

b) Give two examples of changes people can make to their **lifestyle** or **diet** which might reduce their risk of getting cancer.

1. ....

2. ....

Q2 Write numbers in the boxes below to show the correct **order** in which drugs are tested.

☐ Drug is tested on human tissue

☐ Drug is tested on live animals

☐ Human volunteers are used to test the drug

☐ Computer models simulate a response to the drug

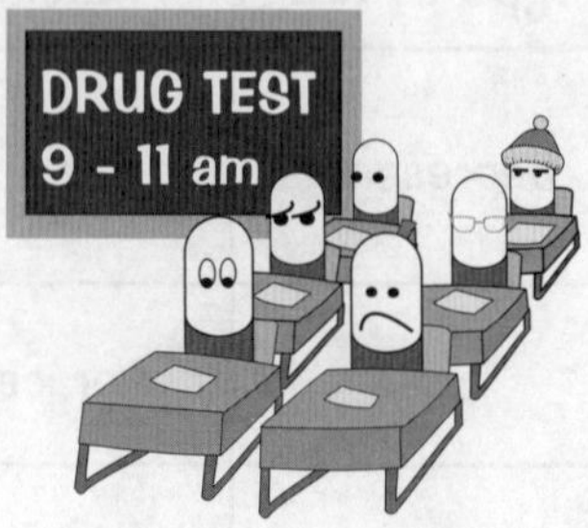

Q3 A pharmaceutical company is trialling a new drug. They are using a **placebo** in the trial and are conducting the trials 'double blind'.

a) What is a placebo?

....

b) Why are the scientists using a placebo?

....

....

c) What is a double blind trial?

....

....

Drugs: Use and Harm

Q1 a) What is a **drug**?

....

b) Some people can become **addicted** to drugs. What does this mean?

....

....

c) Some drugs cause the body to develop a **tolerance** to them. What does this mean?

....

....

Q2 **Complete** the table below, which shows different types of drug and their effects on the body.

Type of drug	Example	Effects
Depressants		
	Paracetamol	Reduce the number of 'painful' stimuli at the nerve endings near an injury
Stimulants		Increase the activity of the brain
	Anabolic steroids	
		Distort what is seen and heard by altering the pathways that the brain sends messages along

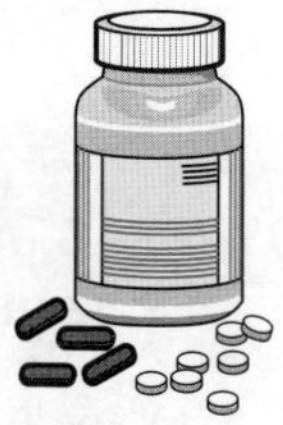

Q3 Three people were arrested and charged with drug offences. Janice had been found taking ketamine (a class C drug). Paul and Duncan had been discovered taking amphetamines (a class B drug). Paul had obtained the drugs and had given some to Duncan.

a) Who is likely to receive the **most** severe punishment? Explain your answer.

....

....

b) Who is likely to receive the **least** severe punishment? Explain your answer.

....

....

Smoking and Alcohol

Q1 Smoking can cause a lot of different **health problems**.

a) Name **one** disease that can be caused by smoking.

....

b) Pregnant women are strongly advised not to smoke.
What effect can smoking have on a baby's birth weight?

....

Q2 **Alcohol** damages the cells in your body.

Describe the effect of excessive alcohol intake on the **liver**.

....

....

....

....

Q3 In the UK, the legal limit for alcohol in the blood when driving is **80 mg per 100 cm³**. The table shows the number of 'units' of alcohol in different drinks. One **unit** increases the blood alcohol level by over **20 mg per 100 cm³** in most people.

DRINK	ALCOHOL UNITS
1 pint of strong lager	3
1 pint of beer	2
1 single measure of whisky	1

a) Bill drinks two pints of strong lager. How many units of alcohol has he had?

....

b) Is Bill's blood alcohol level likely to mean that he cannot legally drive? Explain your answer.

....

....

Assume he drank the pints fairly quickly.

c) Explain why it can be dangerous to drive a car after drinking alcohol.

....

Smoking and Alcohol

Q4 Tick the boxes next to the following statements to show whether they are **true** or **false**.

		True	False
a)	The main effect of alcohol is to increase the activity of the nervous system.	☐	☐
b)	People's coordination, balance and judgement improve when they drink alcohol.	☐	☐
c)	Alcohol causes dehydration, which can damage cells in the brain.	☐	☐

Q5 The graph shows how the number of **smokers** aged between 35 and 54 in the UK has changed since 1950.

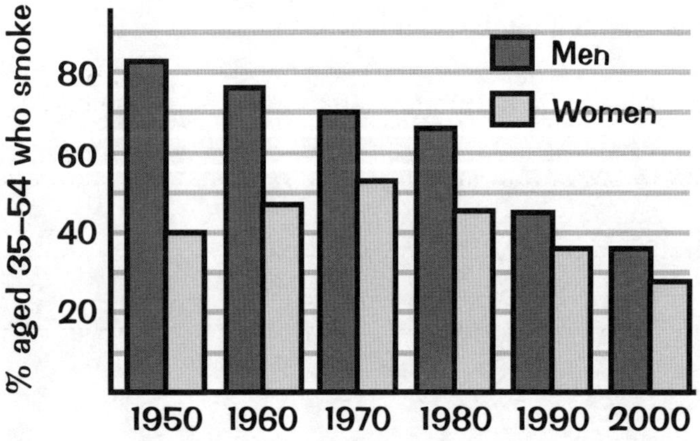

a) What percentage of **men** smoked in 1970?

....

b) Describe the main **trends** you can see in this graph.

....

....

....

....

c) Explain how smoking causes **smoker's cough.**

....

....

....

Top Tips: The facts about what cigarettes and alcohol do to your body are pretty nasty and off-putting. It's good for you to know them, so you can choose a healthy lifestyle.

Receptors — The Eye

Q1 Write **labels** in the spaces to complete the diagram of a human eye.

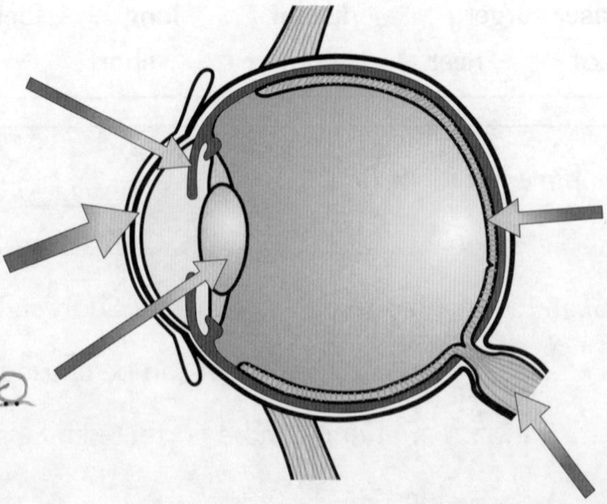

Q2 **Complete the table** about the functions of different parts of the eye.

Part of the eye	Function
cornea X	Focuses light on the retina
optic nerve	Carries impulses from the eye to the brain
Retina	rods + cones
Ciliary muscles	contracts + relaxs to distance
Iris	Controls how much light enters the pupil

Q3 **Circle** the correct word in each pair to complete the passage below.

The eye focuses light by changing the shape of the **elastic** / **rigid lens**.
This is known as **accommodation** / **adaptation**.
When you look at distant objects, your ciliary muscle **contracts** / **relaxes**, and the suspensory ligaments **tighten** / **slacken**. The lens becomes **more rounded** / **less rounded** and light is refracted **more** / **less**. To focus on near objects the opposite actions happen.

Receptors — The Eye

Q4 Fill in the blanks in the paragraph using some of the words from the list below.

corneal laser surgery	distant	long	behind	concave
in front of	near	convex	short	laser hair removal

Long-sighted people can't focus on ....near.................... objects. This can be because their eyeball is too ....short.................... . Glasses or contact lenses with a ....convex.................... lens can correct this problem. Short-sighted people can't focus on ....distant.................... objects. This problem can be caused by a person's eyeball being too ....long.................... , but it can be corrected by glasses or contact lenses with a ....concave.................... lens. ....corneal laser surg.................... is an alternative to glasses and contact lenses to correct long- and short-sightedness.

Q5 The picture below shows a bird with **binocular vision**.

a) **Binocular vision** allows the bird to judge distances well.
Explain how binocular vision works.

....

....

b) Give **one** disadvantage of binocular vision.

....

Q6 Gerald is **colour blind**. This means he has difficulty distinguishing between certain wavelengths of light.

a) Name the part of the eye that contains **light receptors**.

Retina..

b) What is **red-green colour blindness** a result of?

lack of cones..

Neurones and Reflexes

Q1 Circle the correct answer to complete each of the following sentences.

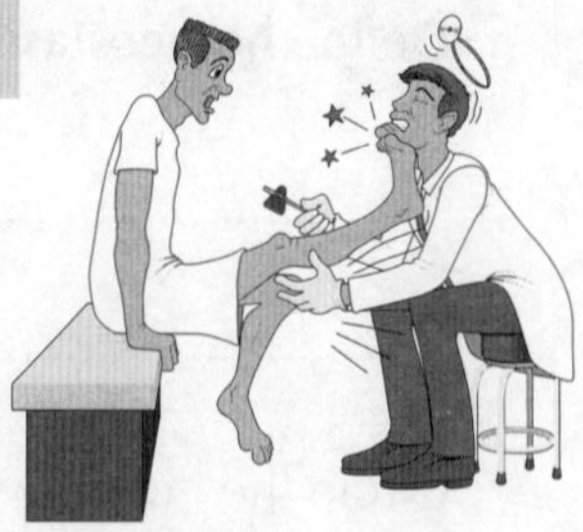

a) Reflexes happen **quickly / slowly**.

b) The main purpose of a reflex is to **protect / display** the body.

c) Reflexes happen **with / without** you thinking about them.

d) The pathway taken by a reflex is called a **reflex arc / reflex curve**.

Q2 Place numbers in the boxes to show the **passage of a reflex**, starting with 'stimulus'.

☐ Response ☐ Sensory neurone ☐ Receptor ☐ Effector

☐ Motor neurone [1] Stimulus ☐ Relay neurone

Q3 The diagram below shows a typical **motor neurone**.

a) How does information travel along the neurone?

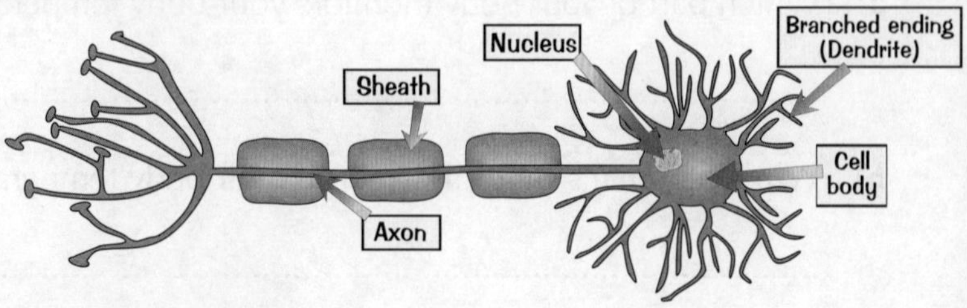

....

....

b) Why is it useful that the end of a neurone is **branched**?

....

c) What is the **function** of the sheath around the axon?

....

....

Q4 The gap between two neurones is called a **synapse**.

a) Explain how the information from a nerve impulse crosses the synapse.

....

b) Describe the effect of **stimulant** drugs on synapses.

....

....

Top Tips: Reflex actions are pretty useful. If your hand falls into a pan of boiling oil, you'll take your hand out **automatically**, rather than keeping it in there while you wonder what to do.

Homeostasis

Q1 Define **homeostasis**.

....

....

Q2 Circle the correct word in each pair to complete the passage below.

> Negative feedback is a response mechanism that **increases** / **counteracts** changes in the body's internal environment. For example, a rise in body temperature causes a response that **raises** / **lowers** body temperature. Negative feedback keeps the internal environment at an **optimum** / **upper** level at which cells can function properly.

Q3 The human body is usually maintained at a **temperature** of about **37 °C**.

a) Which part of your body monitors your body temperature to ensure that it is kept constant?

....

b) Why do humans suffer ill effects if their body temperature varies too much from 37 °C?

....

....

c) Name **one** condition you can get if you're exposed to:

i) **high** temperatures for a long time ....

ii) **low** temperatures for a long time ....

Q4 Your body has various techniques for adjusting body temperature to keep it constant.

a) Explain how **sweating** helps to lower your body temperature.

....

....

b) **i)** Explain what **vasodilation** and **vasoconstriction** are.

....

....

ii) How do vasodilation and vasoconstriction help to keep your body temperature constant?

....

....

Controlling Blood Sugar Level

Q1 Most people's **blood sugar** level is controlled by **homeostasis**.

a) Where does the **sugar** in your blood come from?

....

b) i) Name the **main hormone** involved in the regulation of blood sugar level.

....

ii) The hormone converts excess blood glucose into glycogen.
Name the **organ** where this takes place.

....

Q2 Complete the flow chart to show what happens when the **glucose** level in the blood gets too **high**.

Blood contains too much glucose.

↓

.... is released by the ....

↓

.... makes the .... turn glucose into glycogen for storage.

↓

.... is removed from the ....

↓

Blood glucose level is now ....

Q3 Blood sugar level is controlled by a **hormone**.
Explain why nervous messages are faster than hormonal ones.

....

....

....

Controlling Blood Sugar Level

Q4 Ruby has **type 1 diabetes.**

a) What is type 1 diabetes?

....

....

b) Give two ways in which type 1 diabetics **control** their blood sugar levels.

1. ....

2. ....

c) Ruby injects insulin and then eats a meal.
Describe the effect of the insulin on her blood sugar level.

....

....

....

d) Ruby starts playing hockey three times a week. Will this affect the insulin dosage she requires?
Explain your answer.

....

....

....

Q5 Paul has **type 2 diabetes.**

a) What is type 2 diabetes?

....

....

b) Describe how can Paul control his diabetes.

....

....

Top Tips: Although diabetes is a serious disease, many diabetics are able to control their blood sugar levels and carry on with normal lives. Sir Steve Redgrave even won a gold medal at the Olympics after he had been diagnosed with type 1 diabetes.

Plant Hormones and Growth

Q1 Tick the correct box to show whether the following statements are **true** or **false**.

	True	False
a) Plant shoots grow away from light.		
b) Plant roots grow towards light.		
c) Plant roots grow in the same direction that gravity acts.		
d) If the tip of a shoot is removed, the shoot may stop growing upwards.		

Q2 Choose the correct word or phrase from each pair to complete the following paragraph.

When a shoot tip is exposed to light from one side, auxin accumulates on the side that's in the **light** / **shade**. This makes the cells grow **faster** / **slower** on the shaded side, so the shoot bends **away from** / **towards** the light. This means that shoots are **positively** / **negatively** phototropic. When a root is exposed to light from one side, auxin accumulates on the side that's in the **light** / **shade**. This makes the cells grow **faster** / **slower** on the shaded side, so the root bends **towards** / **away from** the light. This means that roots are **positively** / **negatively** phototropic.

Q3 Two shoot tips were removed from young plants. Agar blocks soaked in **auxin** were placed on the cut ends of the shoots as shown in the diagram, and placed in the dark.

a) Describe how auxin moves through a plant.

....

....

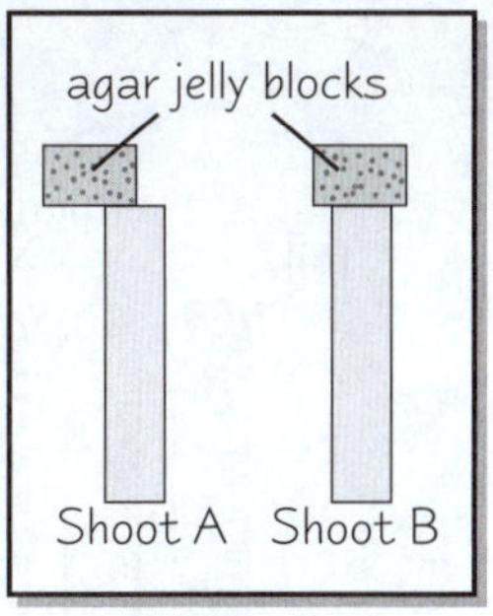

b) Describe the expected responses of shoots A and B to this treatment.

i) Shoot A ....

ii) Shoot B ....

c) Explain your answers.

i) Shoot A ....

....

ii) Shoot B ....

....

Plant Hormones and Growth

Q4 Cedrick placed some **seedlings** on the surface of **damp soil** and left them for **five days**. The appearance of a seedling is shown in the diagram.

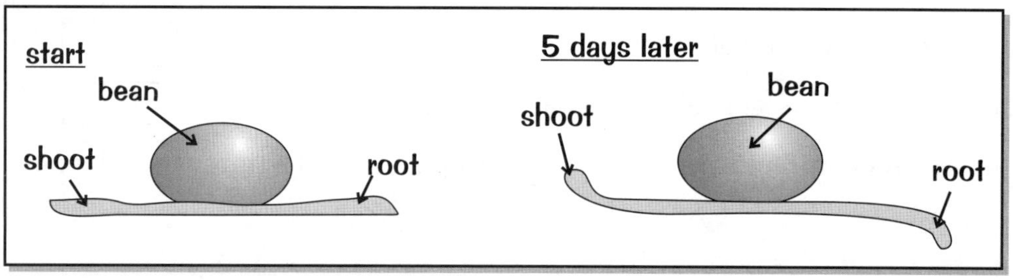

a) What **hormones** are responsible for these changes? ....

b) Where are these hormones produced? ....

c) Explain the responses of the shoot and the root to **gravity**.
For each one, say whether the response was **positively** or **negatively geotropic**.

i) the shoot ....

....

ii) the root ....

....

Q5 Vicky used three seedlings to investigate plant growth. Each seedling was prepared differently (see table). All three were placed in the same conditions, exposed to light from **one** direction and left for five hours. She recorded her results in the table below.

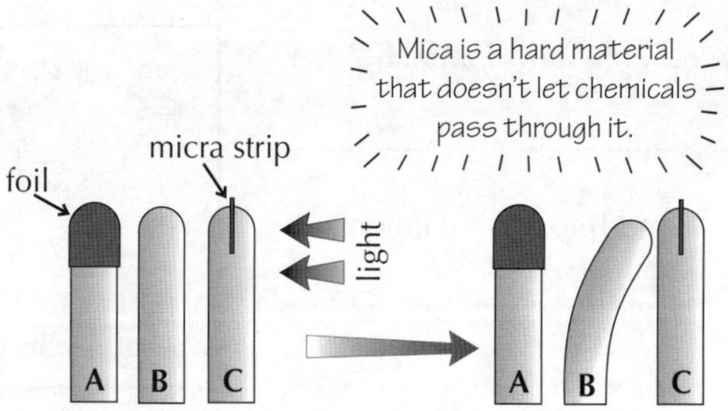

Seedling	Preparation	Observation after 5 hours
A	foil covering tip	no change
B	left alone	tip bent towards the light
C	mica strip through centre of tip	no change

Suggest why seedling A and seedling C failed to respond to the light.

Seedling A ....

....

Seedling C ....

....

Commercial Use of Plant Hormones

Q1 Describe four ways in which **plant hormones** can be used **commercially**.

1. ....

2. ....

3. ....

4. ....

Q2 Ronald owns a fruit farm which grows satsumas. The fruit is picked before it is ripe and transported to market.

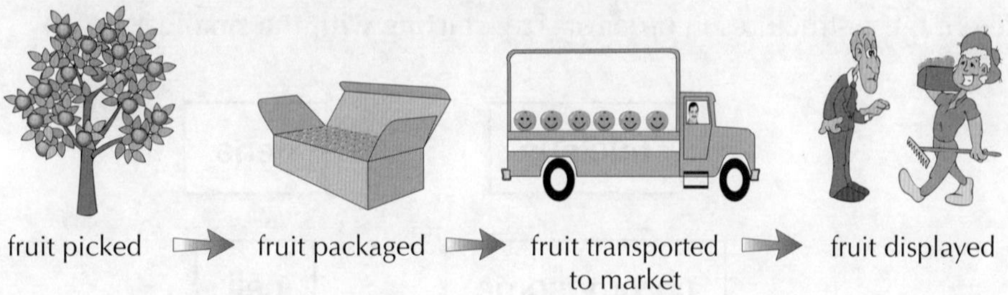

a) Suggest why the satsumas are picked before they are ripe.

....

....

b) **i)** How could the unripened satsumas be ripened in time to reach the market?

....

ii) At what stage in the diagram above should the satsumas be ripened?

....

Q3 Charlie sprayed a batch of **dormant** barley seeds with a dilute solution of a plant hormone. This caused all the seeds to germinate.

a) Define the term **dormancy**.

....

b) Suggest **two** reasons why it is useful to be able to control when seeds germinate.

....

....

Genes and Chromosomes

Q1 Complete the passage by choosing from the words given below.
You can only use each word once.

DNA **nucleus** **gene**
chromosomes **membrane** **organ**

Almost every cell of the body is controlled by a structure called the ....

This structure contains strands of genetic material called ....

They are made of a chemical called .... Each section of genetic material that controls a characteristic is called a ....

Q2 Write out these structures in order of size, **starting with the smallest.**

nucleus **gene**

chromosome **cell**

....

Q3 Tick the correct boxes to show whether each statement is **true** or **false**.

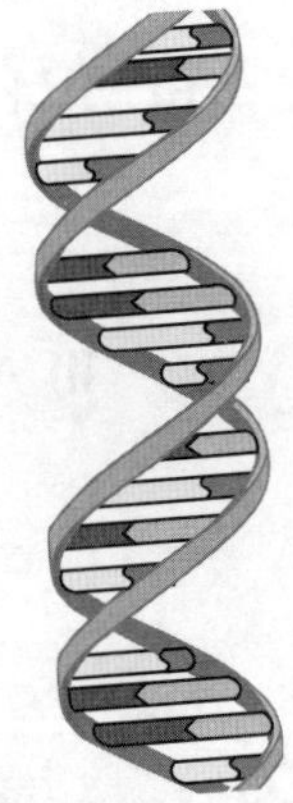

	True	False
a) Human body cells contain 44 chromosomes.	☐	☐
b) Chromosomes are long lengths of DNA.	☐	☐
c) In most animal cells, chromosomes come in pairs.	☐	☐
d) All species have the same number of chromosomes.	☐	☐

Q4 Which of the following is the correct definition of the term '**alleles**'? Underline your choice.

'Alleles' is the collective term for all the genes found on a pair of chromosomes.

'Alleles' are different forms of the same gene.

'Alleles' are identical organisms produced by asexual reproduction.

Top Tips: You need to know exactly what's meant by genes, alleles, DNA, chromosomes, etc. Once you understand all that, you'll be ready to get your head around the rest of this genetics malarkey.

Genetic Variation

Q1 Complete the table by putting a tick in the correct box. The first one has been done for you.

	Can cause variation	Does not cause variation
Formation of gametes from reproductive cells	✓	
Mutation of a reproductive cell		
Random fertilisation		
Conditions in the womb when the baby is developing		
Environmental effects after birth		

Q2 **One** of the statements below is **true**. Tick the box next to the correct one.

1. Neither your genes nor your environment are important in determining any of your attributes. ☐
2. Your health is only determined by your genes. ☐
3. Your environment is the most important factor for your sporting ability. ☐
4. It's hard to say if your genes or your environment are more important for characteristics like intelligence. ☐

Q3 The formation of gametes and fertilisation both cause **genetic variation.**

a) **i)** What are gametes? ....

ii) Explain how the formation of gametes results in genetic variation.

....

....

b) Explain how fertilisation causes genetic variation.

....

....

c) Most human body cells have **46** chromosomes.
Explain why gametes need to have **23** chromosomes..

....

....

Genetic Diagrams

Q1 a) Are both versions of an allele always expressed?

....

b) When looking at a genetic diagram, how can you tell which is the dominant allele and which is the recessive allele?

....

....

c) An organism with two of the same alleles for a characteristic is known as what?

....

Q2 A type of fly usually has **red** eyes. However, there are a small number of white-eyed flies. Having **white** eyes is a **recessive** characteristic.

a) Complete the following sentences with either '**red eyes**' or '**white eyes**'.

i) **R** is the allele for ....

ii) **r** is the allele for ....

iii) Flies with alleles **RR** or **Rr** will have ....

iv) Flies with the alleles **rr** will have ....

b) Two flies have the alleles **Rr**. They fall in love and get it on.

i) Complete this genetic diagram to show the alleles of the possible offspring. One's been done for you.

	parent's alleles: R	parent's alleles: r
parent's alleles: R	RR	
parent's alleles: r		

ii) What is the probability that any one of the flies' offspring will have white eyes?

....

iii) The flies have 96 offspring. How many of the offspring are **likely** to have **red eyes**?

....

Genetic Diagrams

Q3 Draw lines to match each word to its **definition**.

Genotype	The characteristics expressed by an organism.
Phenotype	The genetic makeup of an organism.

Q4 An allele for the colour grey (**G**) in mice is dominant over the allele for the colour white (**g**). A heterozygous grey mouse (**Gg**) was bred with a homozygous white mouse (**gg**).

a) Complete the genetic diagram below to show the potential combinations of alleles in the offspring of the two mice.

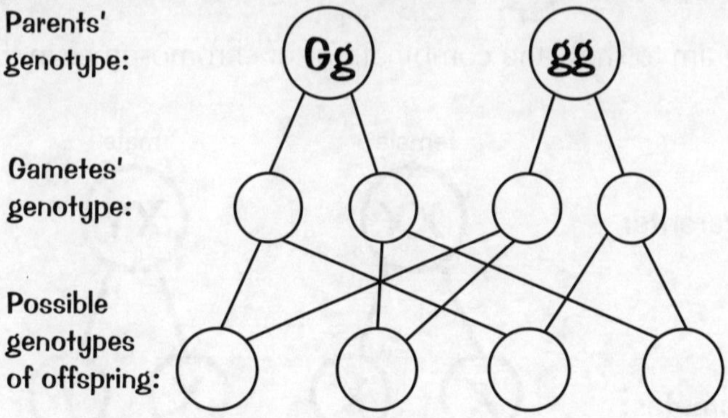

b) What is the likely ratio of colours in any offspring (grey : white)?

c) If the mice had 12 babies, how many would there most **likely** be of each colour?

Q5 Sally is investigating the inheritance of **flower colours**. She knows that the allele for the colour **red** is **dominant** and the allele for the colour **white** is **recessive**.

Sally has two of the same plant, one with **red** flowers and one with **white** flowers. Suggest how Sally can find out whether the red-flowered plant is homozygous red (**RR**) or heterozygous red (**Rr**).

Sex Inheritance and Genetic Disorders

Q1 Tick the boxes to show whether each statement is **true** or **false**.

		True	False
a)	Women have two X chromosomes. Men have an X and a Y chromosome.	☐	☐
b)	There is a 75% chance that a couple's first child will be a girl.	☐	☐
c)	Sperm cells (male gametes) can carry an X or a Y chromosome.	☐	☐
d)	If the first born is a girl, the second born will always be a boy.	☐	☐

Q2 Here is a genetic diagram showing the inheritance of **sex chromosomes** in humans.

a) Complete the diagram to show the combinations of chromosomes in the offspring.

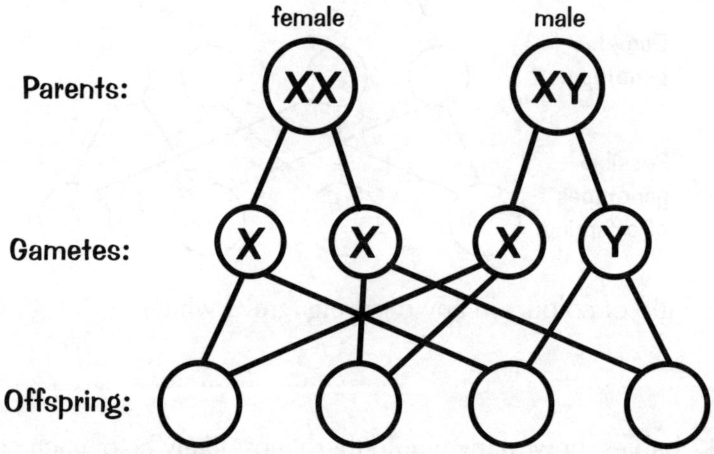

b) A woman becomes pregnant. What is the probability that the embryo is **male**?

....

c) Sarah says, "If I have eight children, four of them will definitely be boys."
Is Sarah right? Explain your answer.

....

....

....

Top Tips: The way the X and Y chromosomes are passed on is a nifty way of ensuring roughly equal numbers of men and women are born. Pretty useful for the survival of the species, I'd say.

Sex Inheritance and Genetic Disorders

Q3 **Cystic fibrosis** is a genetic (inherited) disorder that is caused by a **recessive allele**.

a) How many copies of the allele do you need to be:

Carriers of genetic disorders don't show symptoms.

i) a **carrier** of cystic fibrosis?

....

ii) a **suffer** of cystic fibrosis?

....

b) Complete the following genetic diagram showing the inheritance of cystic fibrosis.

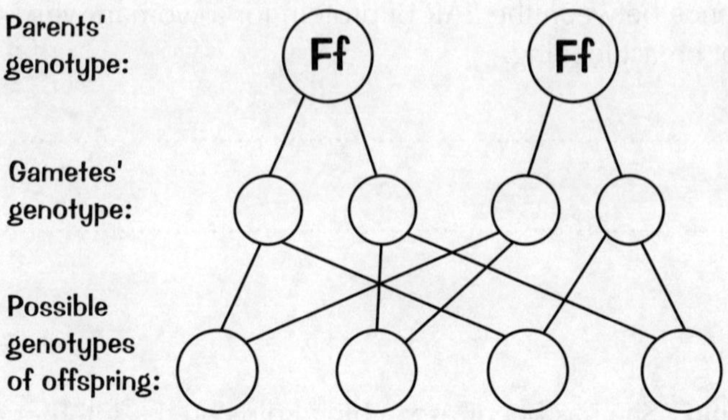

c) **i)** In the above genetic diagram, what is the probability of a child having cystic fibrosis?

....

ii) In the above genetic diagram, what is the probability of a child being a **carrier** of the cystic fibrosis allele (but not having the disease)?

....

Q4 Sarah and Ahmad are expecting a baby. Tests have revealed that there is a **high chance** the baby will have a **genetic disorder** that could result in death within its first year of life. They have to decide whether to terminate the pregnancy.

a) Give **one** argument that could be used in **favour** of a termination of the pregnancy.

....

....

b) Give **one** argument that could be used **against** a termination of the pregnancy.

....

....

Mixed Questions — Module B1

Q1 **Protein** is one of six nutrients that help your body to function properly.

a) What are proteins made from? Circle the correct answer from the choice of words below.

amino acids glycerol fatty acids proteases

b) Where are proteins stored in the body?

....

c) What condition is likely to develop in people whose diets don't have enough protein?

....

d) Explain the difference between the EAR of protein for a woman who is breast feeding and a woman who is not breast feeding.

....

....

Q2 Josephine has a **cold**. She has been researching colds on the internet and she has read that they are caused by **viruses**. Josephine has also read about an experimental drug that could be used to fight off infections like colds.

a) Could an **antibiotic** be used to clear up Josephine's cold? Explain your answer.

....

b) The experimental drug that Josephine read about is currently being tested on animals. It is due to be tested in a blind trial in a few months.

i) Suggest one way that the drug might have been tested before being tested on animals.

....

ii) Suggest one reason why people might object to animal testing.

....

iii) What is a blind trial?

....

....

Top Tips: These mixed questions are kind of like the questions you'll get in your exam — each one could cover a variety of topics from the whole module, just to keep you on your toes...

Mixed Questions — Module B1

Q3 The diagram below shows how the **blood sugar level** is controlled in humans.

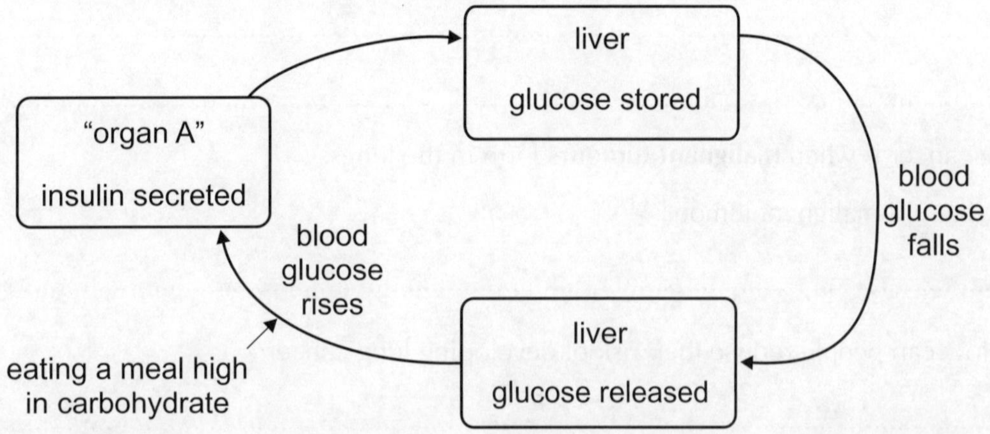

a) Name **'organ A'** in the diagram above.

....

b) Complete the following sentence:

Excess glucose is removed from your blood and stored in the liver as ....

c) Explain how the diagram shows an example of **negative feedback**.

....

....

Q4 Some people are **red-green colour blind** — this means that they can't tell the difference between red and green objects.

a) Tick the box next to the statement that is **true**.

1. Red-green colour blindness results from having too many cone cells in the retina. ☐
2. Red-green colour blindness results from a lack of specialised cone cells in the retina. ☐
3. Red-green colour blindness results from a problem with the optic nerve. ☐
4. Red-green colour blindness results from the lens being the wrong shape. ☐

b) Red-green colour blindness is caused by a recessive allele.

i) What are alleles?

....

ii) When are the characteristics of a recessive allele expressed?

....

Mixed Questions — Module B1

Q5 a) Suggest why smokers are more likely to suffer from **lung cancer** than non-smokers.

....

....

b) Lung cancer is when **malignant tumours** form in the lungs.

i) What is a malignant tumour?

....

ii) How can people reduce their risk of developing lung cancer?

....

Q6 Albinism is a genetic condition. Affected people, called albinos, lack any skin pigmentation. A couple, neither of whom is albino, have a child who is an albino.

Is the allele for albinism **dominant** or **recessive**? Explain your answer.

....

....

Q7 Sex determination in chickens is different from in humans. Male chickens (cockerels) have two Z chromosomes and females (hens) have ZW chromosomes.

a) Apart from having different letters, explain how this differs from human sex determination.

....

....

b) Complete the genetic diagram to show how sex is determined in chickens.

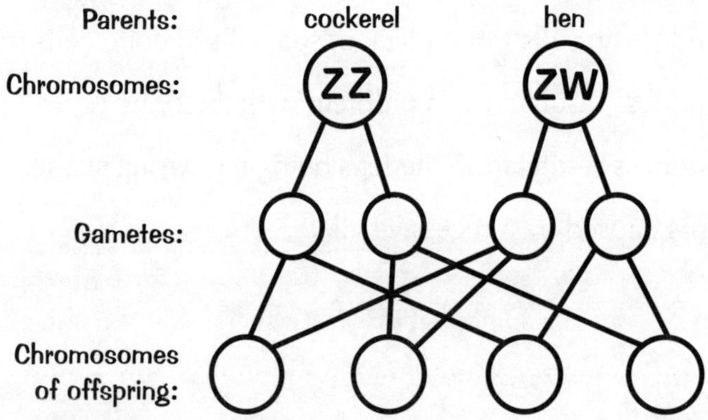

You don't need to know anything about chickens to answer this question — just apply what you already know about sex determination in humans.

c) What is the probability of any one fertilised chicken's egg developing into a cockerel?

....

Classification

Q1 a) Organisms can be **classified** into different groups. Fill in the missing labels on the diagram to show the names of the different groups.

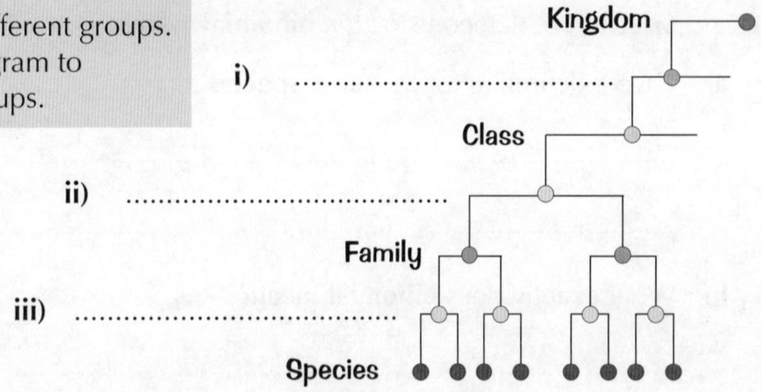

b) Describe the difference between **natural** and **artificial** classification systems.

....

....

c) Explain why it can be difficult to classify living organisms into distinct groups.

....

Q2 Complete the following passage to explain why **classification systems change** over time. The words you need are in the box below.

genetic	classification	sequencing	species	adapted	related

Sometimes when a new .... is discovered it doesn't really fit into any of the groups in the existing .... system. As a result, the system has to be .... to include the new species. DNA .... of species that we already know lots about can show us .... differences between different groups. This data might change our minds about how closely .... two groups of organisms are — causing us to change how we classify them.

Q3 Use the information in the passage to **label** the **evolutionary tree** below with the letters A-D.

A and B are fossilised bones from the legs of ancestors of the modern horse. Some scientists believe that animals with legs like fossil A gradually developed into animals with legs like fossil B. It is thought that there was a stage in the development of the horse between A and B, during which the leg bone would have looked like C. Animals with legs like fossil D are closely related to animals with legs like fossil B. But, those animals with legs like fossil D aren't direct ancestors of the modern horse.

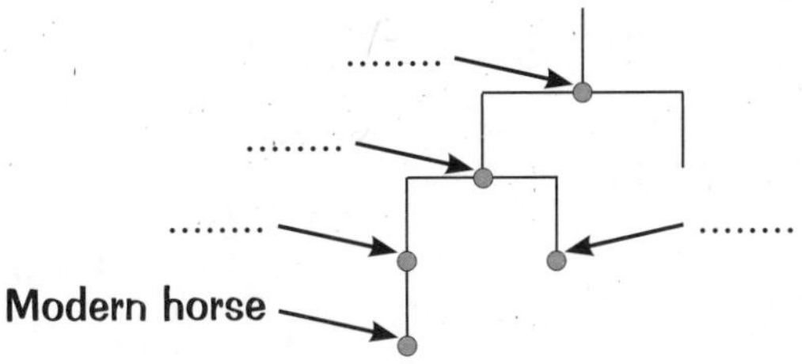

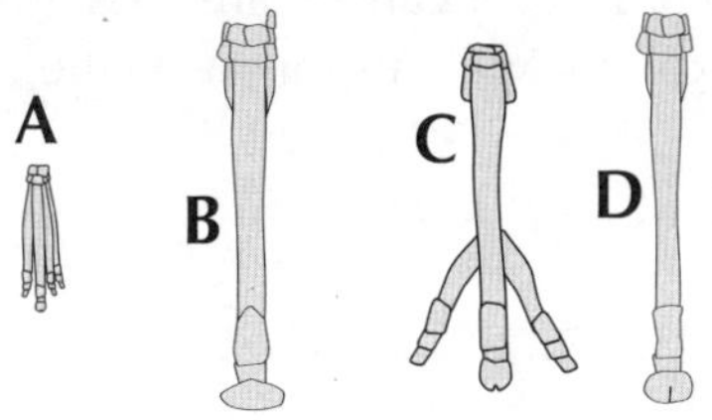

Species

Q1 **Species** are named using the **binomial system**.

a) Give a definition for the term '**species**'.

....

....

b) What exactly does **binomial** mean?

....

c) The binomial name for humans is *Homo sapiens*.
Which part of the name refers to the species that humans belong to?

....

Q2 Donkeys and horses are different **species**. When a donkey and a horse reproduce the resulting offspring is a **mule**. Give **one** problem with classifying hybrid organisms like the mule into species.

....

....

Q3 Dave thinks he's discovered a new species of bacterium, but he isn't sure. Bacteria **reproduce asexually**. Explain why this makes it difficult to classify bacteria into species.

....

....

Q4 a) Explain how comparing the **common ancestors** of two species can tell us how **closely related** the species are.

....

....

b) **Llamas** and **camels** are closely related, but they look very different.
Explain why this might be the case.

....

....

Pyramids of Biomass and Numbers

Q1 The following diagram shows a garden food chain. The **number** and **dry biomass** of the organisms at each stage in the food chain is shown below.

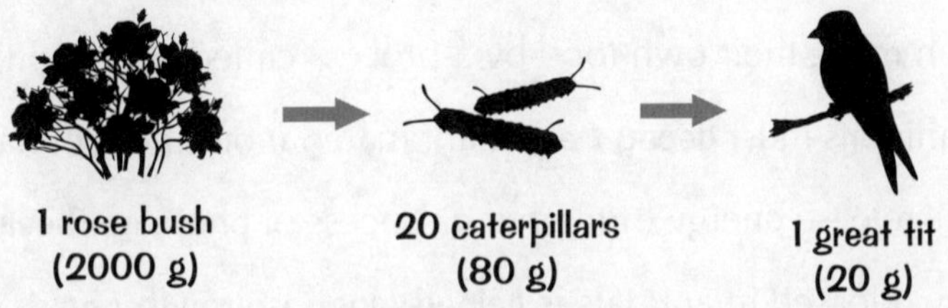

a) Draw and label a **pyramid of biomass** for the food chain in the grid below. Each **large** square of the grid should represent **200 grams**.

b) Explain why a **pyramid of numbers** for this food chain would be a **different shape** to the pyramid of biomass you've drawn above.

....

....

Q2 Drawing pyramids of biomass is not always straightforward.

a) To construct a pyramid of biomass, you have to measure the **dry biomass** of the organisms in a food chain.

i) What is dry biomass?

....

ii) Give **one** reason why measuring dry biomass can be difficult.

....

b) Give **one** other reason why it can be difficult to construct pyramids of biomass.

....

....

Energy Transfer and Energy Flow

Q1 Complete the sentences below by circling the correct words.

a) Nearly all life on Earth depends on **food** / **energy** from the Sun.

b) **Plants** / **Animals** can make their own food by a process called **photosynthesis** / **respiration**.

c) To obtain energy animals must **decay** / **eat** plant material or other animals.

d) Animals and plants release energy through the process of **photosynthesis** / **respiration**.

e) Some of the energy released in animals is **gained** / **lost** as **growth** / **heat** before it reaches organisms at later steps of the food chain.

Q2 A **food chain** is shown in the diagram.

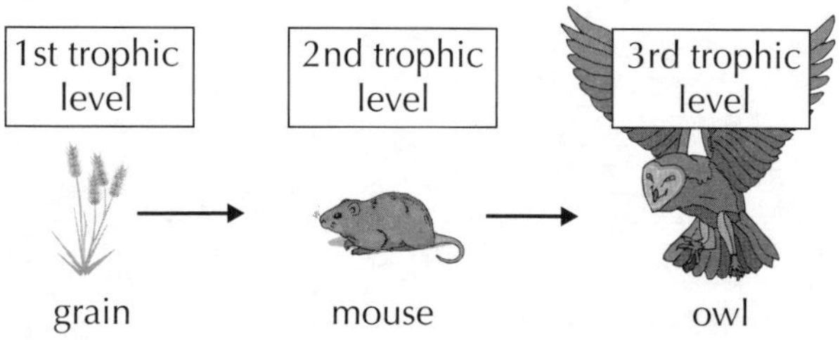

a) Put the following amounts of energy under the correct organisms.

500 kJ, 50 000 kJ, 8000 kJ

b) Calculate the amount of energy lost between the:

i) 1st and 2nd trophic levels. ....

ii) 2nd and 3rd trophic levels. ....

c) Calculate the efficiency of energy transfer from the:

i) 1st to 2nd trophic level. ....

ii) 2nd to 3rd trophic level. ....

Q3 Study the diagram of **energy transfer** shown.

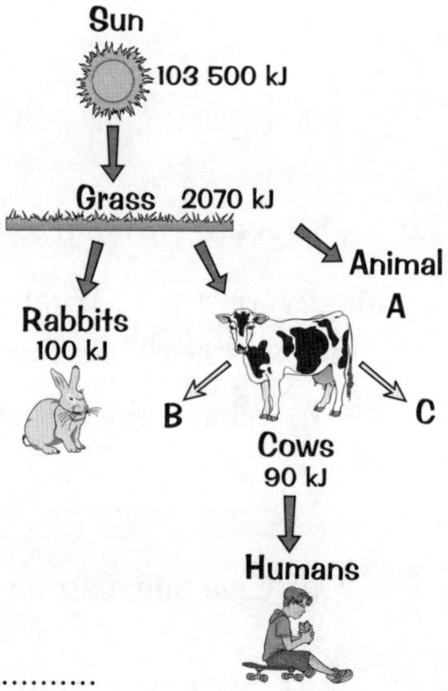

a) Using the figures shown on the diagram, work out the percentage of the Sun's energy that is available in the grass.

....

b) The efficiency of energy transfer from the grass to the next trophic level is 10%. Work out how much energy is available in animal A.

....

c) **B** and **C** are processes that represent energy loss. Suggest what these processes might be.

....

d) Why do food chains rarely have more than five trophic levels?

....

....

Energy Transfer and Energy Flow

Q4 Another **food chain** is shown below.

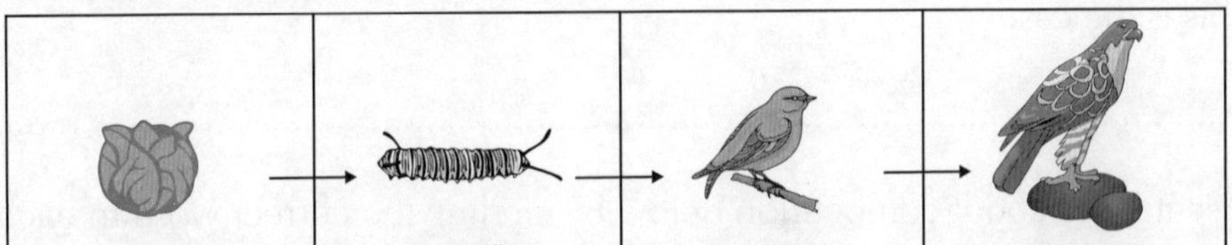

	lettuce	Caterpillar	small bird	large bird
1	10 kJ	100 kJ	5000 kJ	30 000 kJ
2	30 000 kJ	30 000 kJ	30 000 kJ	30 000 kJ
3	30 000 kJ	5000 kJ	100 kJ	10 kJ

a) Which row, 1, 2 or 3, shows the amount of energy available at each trophic level? ....

b) Circle the answer below that shows how much energy is available to the caterpillar.

5000 kJ   25 000 kJ   30 000 kJ

c) Circle the answer below that shows how much energy is lost from the caterpillar to the small bird.

100 kJ   4900 kJ   5000 kJ

Q5 An **aquatic food chain** is shown.

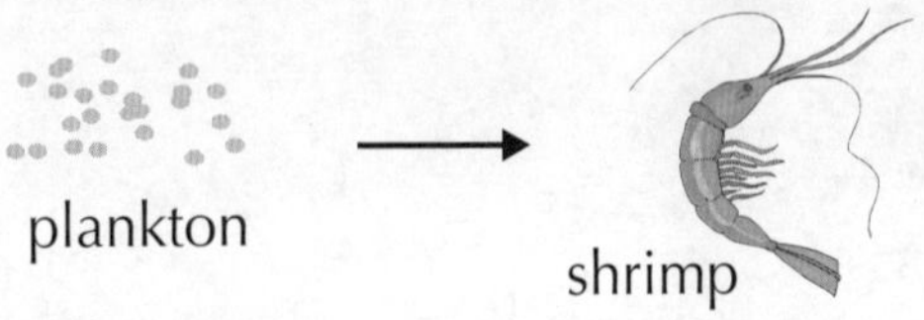

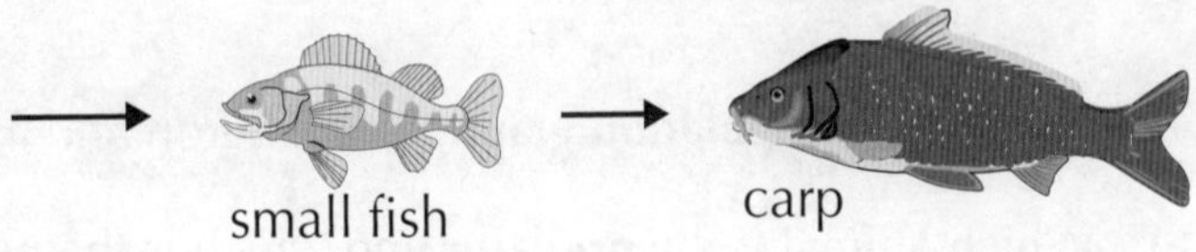

100 000 kJ   ....   1000 kJ   ....

a) 90 000 kJ is lost between the 1st trophic level (plankton) and the 2nd trophic level (shrimp).

i) On the diagram, write the amount of energy available in the shrimp for the small fish.

ii) Calculate the **efficiency** of energy transfer from the 1st to the 2nd trophic level.

....

b) The energy transfer from the small fish to the carp is **5%** efficient.

i) On the diagram, write the amount of **energy** available in the **carp**.

ii) How much energy is **lost** from the food chain at this stage?

....

c) A **pyramid of biomass** is drawn for this food chain. Explain why it is pyramid shaped.

....

....

Interactions Between Organisms

Q1 **Similar organisms** living in the same habitat are often in **close competition** for resources.

a) Explain why this is the case.

....

b) Complete the sentences about competition below by circling the correct word in each pair.

i) **Intraspecific** / **Interspecific** competition is where organisms compete for resources against individuals of another species.

ii) **Intraspecific** / **Interspecific** competition is where organisms compete for resources against individuals of the same species.

iii) Intraspecific competition often has a **smaller** / **bigger** impact on organisms than interspecific competition.

Q2 Explain what is meant by the term '**ecological niche**'.

....

....

Q3 Look at the **population graph** for the heron and frog.

a) Which animal is the **predator** and which is the **prey**?

Predator: .... Prey: ....

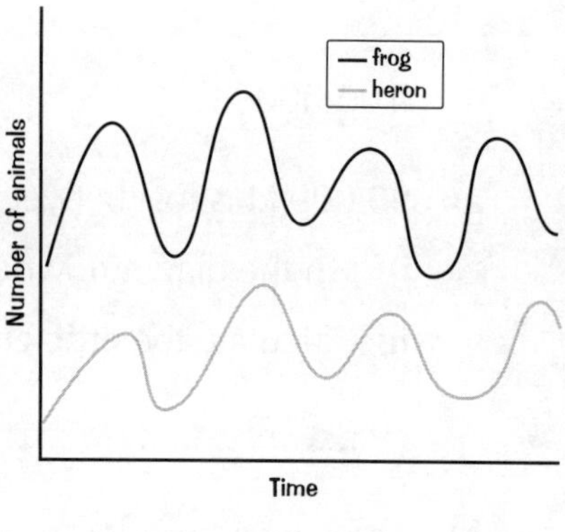

b) Shortly after an increase in the number of herons, what happens to the number of frogs?

....

c) Name two factors that will **reduce** the frog population.

1. .... 2. ....

d) If the frogs run out of food, what will happen to the number of herons?

....

e) Explain why predator-prey population cycles are always out of phase with each other.

....

....

Interactions Between Organisms

Q4 Some organisms, such as **parasites**, depend entirely on other species for their survival.

a) **Two** of the organisms below are parasites. Circle the correct two.

Flea

Tapeworm

~~Tiddles~~

Bumble bee

b) What is the difference between a **parasitic** relationship and **mutualism**?

....

....

c) i) State one example of **mutualism**. ....

ii) Explain why your answer to part **i)** is an example of mutualism.

....

....

iii) Suggest how the **interdependence** of the species in your answer to part **i)** could affect their **abundance**.

....

....

Q5 Read the passage below and answer the questions that follow.

Barn owls compete with each other for mates, hunting territories, nesting sites and food. Foxes and barn owls feed on many of the same species of small mammal. They compete with each other for food, but nothing else.

a) Is the competition between **foxes** and **barn owls** intraspecific or interspecific?

....

b) Which type of competition will have a **bigger impact** on the **barn owl population**?

....

c) Explain your answer to part **b)**.

....

....

Adaptations

Q1 Animals and plants are **adapted** to their environments.

a) Explain what is meant by the term '**adaptation**'.

....

....

b) Explain why animals and plants need to adapt to their environment.

....

....

Q2 Complete these sentences by inserting the word '**generalists**' or '**specialists**' into the gaps.

a) .... are highly adapted to survive in a specific habitat.

b) .... are adapted to survive in a range of different habitats.

c) In a habitat with stable conditions .... will out compete ....

d) In a habitat with changing conditions .... will out compete ....

Q3 a) Complete the paragraph about organisms that are adapted to live in **extreme conditions** using some of the words in the box below.

extremophobes	enzymes	optimum	optical	extremophiles	denature

Some organisms are adapted to survive in extreme conditions. Organisms that are adapted to survive in the most extreme conditions are called .... For example, bacteria that live in extremely hot environments have .... with very high .... temperatures. These temperatures would .... the enzymes of most other organisms.

b) Organisms that live in extremely **cold environments** often produce special '**antifreeze proteins**'. What are 'antifreeze proteins'?

....

....

Adaptations to Cold Environments

Q1 **Fur seals** are adapted to survive in **very cold conditions**.

a) Apart from having a thick furry coat, suggest **one** other anatomical adaptation that might insulate the fur seal's body and trap heat in.

....

b) Fur seals have a **large size** and a **compact body shape**. Does this give them a small or a large **surface area to volume ratio**? Tick the box next to the correct answer below.

small surface area to volume ratio		large surface area to volume ratio	

c) Explain how their surface area to volume ratio helps fur seals survive in cold conditions.

....

....

Q2 The diagram shows a **counter-current heat exchange system** in the leg of a seagull.

a) Explain how the counter-current heat exchange system reduces the amount of heat that the seagull loses to the environment.

....

....

....

....

....

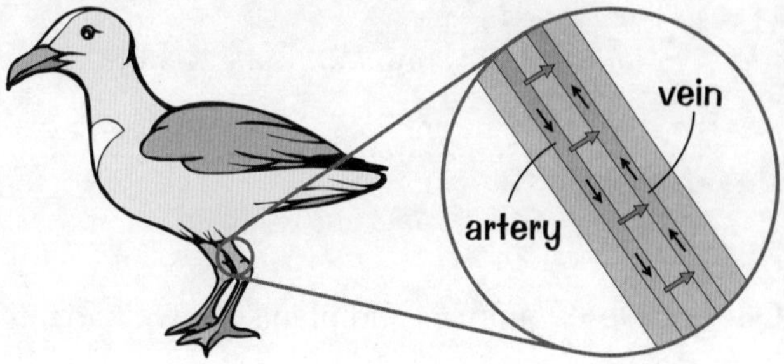

b) Name **one** other organism that has a counter-current heat exchange system.

....

Q3 **Hibernation** is a behavioural adaptation to **cold environments**. Explain how hibernation helps animals in cold environments to **survive**.

....

....

....

Adaptations to Hot and Dry Environments

Q1 Complete the sentences below about **adaptations to hot environments** by circling the correct word(s) from each pair.

a) To keep cool in warm environments, organisms need to **increase** / **reduce** heat gain and **increase** / **reduce** heat loss.

b) Being active at night is **a behavioural** / **an anatomical** adaptation to living in a hot climate.

c) Some animals spend the day in the shade or underground to reduce the amount of heat their bodies **gain from** / **lose to** their surroundings.

d) Having a **small** / **large** surface area to volume ratio helps an animal to lose heat to its surroundings.

Q2 Margaret is looking at some photos of **elephants** that her uncle took on a trip to South Africa.

Margaret asks her biology teacher why the elephants' ears are so large.

Her teacher says that the elephants' large ears are an adaptation which helps them to **lose heat**.

Suggest how having large ears could help elephants to lose heat.

....

....

Q3 Desert animals and plants are well adapted to living in **dry conditions**.

a) Give **one** adaptation that helps **animals** to survive in dry environments.

....

b) i) Give **one** adaptation that helps **plants** to survive in dry environments.

....

ii) Explain how your answer to part **i)** helps the plants to survive.

....

....

Top Tips: Whenever you're thinking about adaptations to dry environments, all you need to think about is water — organisms need to get as much (and lose as little) of it as they can.

Evolution and Speciation

Q1 Giraffes used to have much **shorter** necks than they do today.

The statements below give an explanation, according to Darwin's theory, of how their neck length changed. Write numbers in the boxes to show the **order** the statements should be in.

☐ The giraffes competed for food from low branches. This food started to become scarce. Many giraffes died before they could breed.

☐ More long-necked giraffes survived to breed, so more giraffes were born with long necks.

☐ A giraffe was born with a longer neck than normal. The long-necked giraffe was able to eat more food.

☐ All giraffes had short necks.

☐ The long-necked giraffe survived to have lots of offspring that all had longer necks.

☐ All giraffes have long necks.

Q2 Darwin's theory of natural selection wasn't perfect. Use the words in the box below to complete the paragraph explaining how Darwin's theory was **developed**.

DNA	appeared	inherit	Successful	offspring

Darwin's theory couldn't explain why new characteristics .... or how beneficial adaptations were passed from parents to their ....

We now know that adaptations are controlled by an organism's ....

.... adaptations are passed on to offspring in the genes that they .... from their parents.

Q3 The development of new species is called **speciation**. Speciation requires **reproductive isolation**.

a) What is 'reproductive isolation'?

....

b) Explain how the **geographic isolation** of two populations can lead to reproductive isolation.

....

....

....

....

Theories of Evolution

Q1 Lamarck had a different theory of evolution to Darwin.

a) What was Lamarck's theory of evolution?

....

....

....

b) Explain why Lamarck's ideas were rejected.

....

....

....

Q2 Darwin knew that his theory would stir up some **trouble**, so he didn't publish his work for a long time.

a) Which group of people were particularly upset about Darwin's theory of natural selection?

....

b) Explain why these people were offended by Darwin's theory.

....

....

Q3 Darwin's theory of natural selection is now **widely accepted** as the best explanation of evolution.

Give two reasons why this is the case.

1. ....

....

2. ....

....

Top Tips: You might've thought that all this stuff about Darwin upsetting people was just a bit of background information, but it could come up in the exam — so make sure you don't skip through it when you're revising. It's just as important as understanding what Darwin's theory actually was.

The Carbon Cycle and Decomposition

Q1 Follow the instructions below to complete the diagram of part of the **carbon cycle**.

a) Add an arrow or arrows labelled **P** to represent **photosynthesis**.

b) Add an arrow or arrows labelled **R** to represent **respiration**.

c) Add an arrow or arrows labelled **F** to represent **feeding**.

CO_2 in the air

plant **animal**

Q2 **Carbon** is a very important element that is constantly being recycled.

a) What is the one way that carbon is removed from the atmosphere?

b) In what form is carbon removed from the atmosphere?

c) What is this carbon converted into by plants?

d) How is this carbon passed on through the food chain?

e) By what process do **all** living organisms return carbon to the air?

Q3 The **rate** at which carbon is recycled depends on the **conditions** in the soil.

a) **i)** How would the rate of carbon recycling be different in a **waterlogged** soil, compared to a **well-drained** soil?

ii) Explain your answer to part **i)**.

b) Explain why the **acidity** of the soil would also affect the rate of recycling.

The Carbon Cycle and Decomposition

Q4 Carbon can also be recycled in the **oceans**. Complete the paragraph below about carbon in the oceans using some of the words from the box.

carbon dioxide	water	carbon sinks	granite	atmosphere	limestone
storms	carbonates	rocks	volcanic eruptions	carbon houses	

The oceans absorb huge volumes of .... They act as massive stores of carbon called .... Many species of marine organisms also store carbon in shells made out of .... When the organisms die, these shells fall to the ocean floor. Over a long period of time, the shells slowly form .... rocks. After weathering or .... , the carbon from these rocks is released back into the ....

Q5 The diagram below shows a version of the **carbon cycle**.

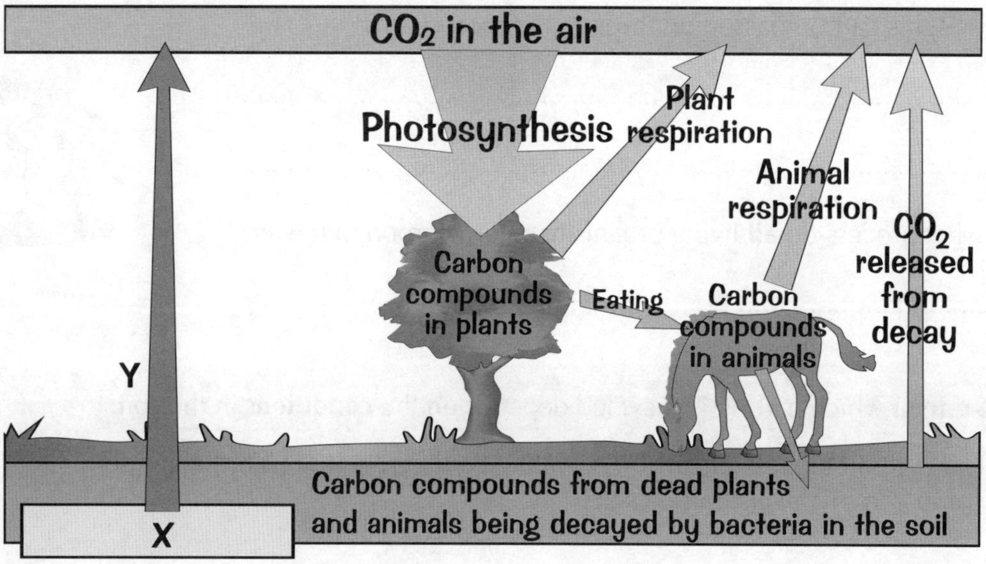

a) Name substance **X** shown on the diagram above. ....

b) Explain why substance **X** contains carbon.

....

....

c) Name the process labelled **Y** on the diagram above. ....

Top Tips: Carbon's super important. Thankfully all that carbon we release from respiration is recycled when plants photosynthesise. They take in the carbon and use it again to make fats, proteins and carbohydrates — which then get passed along the food chain to us. Make sure you can do all the questions on these pages before your exam — the carbon cycle's a favourite topic for examiners.

The Nitrogen Cycle

Q1 Match up each type of **organism** below with the way it obtains **nitrogen**.

Plants	By breaking down dead organisms and animal waste
Animals	By absorbing nitrates from the soil
Decomposers	By eating other organisms

Q2 The nitrogen cycle is dependent on a number of different types of **bacteria**. Explain the role of each of the following types of bacteria in the nitrogen cycle.

Type of bacteria	Role in the nitrogen cycle
a) Decomposers	....
b) Nitrifying bacteria	....
c) Denitrifying bacteria	....
d) Nitrogen-fixing bacteria	....

Q3 Below is a diagram of the **nitrogen cycle**. Explain what is shown in the stages labelled:

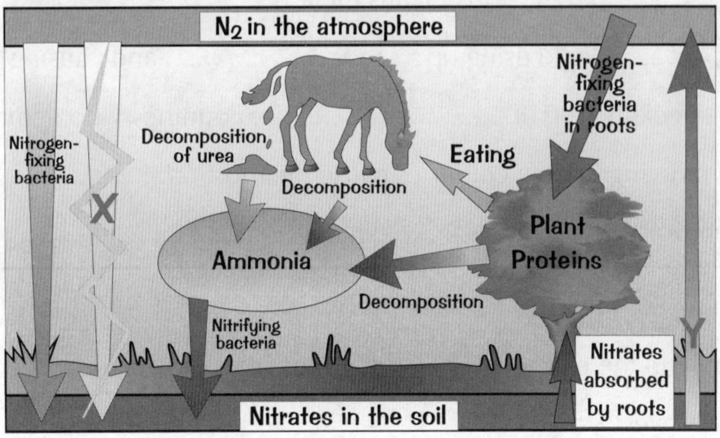

a) X ....

....

....

b) Y ....

....

....

Q4 A farmer was told that if he planted **legume plants** his soil would become more **fertile**.

a) Explain how the legume plants would increase the fertility of his soil.

....

....

b) Explain how this would improve plant growth.

....

....

Human Impact on the Environment

Q1 **Pollution** from human activities has been shown to cause lots of problems for the environment.

a) Give **one** cause of acid rain.

....

b) Suggest **one** consequence of global warming.

....

c) Define the term '**carbon footprint**'.

....

....

Q2 Complete the passage by choosing the correct words from the list below.

Some words can be used more than once.

exponentially   slowly   more   developed   higher   lower
poor   less   pollution   resources   environment   population   developing

Populations increase when birth rate is .... than death rate. The world's population is increasing .... This means there is .... pressure on the .... We're using up .... and causing .... This is especially true of .... countries who demand a .... standard of living. These countries cause the most ...., but have a relatively small proportion of the world's ....

Q3 In 1985, scientists discovered a **hole** in the **ozone layer** above Antarctica.

a) What caused the hole in the ozone layer?

....

....

b) Suggest why scientists studying the hole above Antarctica today should wear sunscreen if they are working outdoors.

....

c) Suggest **one** other possible consequence of the hole in the ozone layer.

....

....

Human Impact on the Environment

Q4 Mayfly larvae and sludgeworms can be studied to see how much **sewage** is in water.

a) What is the name for an organism used in this way? ....

Juanita recorded the number of each species in water samples taken at three different distances away from a sewage outlet. Her results are shown below.

Distance (km)	No. of mayfly larvae	No. of sludgeworms
1	3	20
2	11	14
3	23	7

b) What can you conclude about the two organisms from these results?

....

....

Q5 Dave is investigating the local air quality. He collects data on the **sulfur dioxide concentration** in the air at different sites in his town. His data is shown in the table below.

Site	sulfur dioxide concentration (micrograms/m^3)
1	9.8
2	9.4
3	7.1

a) At which site is the sulfur dioxide concentration the **highest**?

....

b) Dave measured the sulfur dioxide concentration directly, using specialist equipment. Give one advantage and one disadvantage of using **non-living methods** to measure pollution.

Advantage: ....

Disadvantage: ....

c) **i)** Give an example of an **indicator species** that could be used to monitor **air quality**.

....

ii) Suggest **one** reason why Dave did not use indicator species in his study.

....

....

Endangered Species

Q1 Fill in the gaps, choosing from the words below. You might not need all the words.

restrictions ensuring medicines conservation undiscovered television endangered plants extinct

.... programmes often benefit much more than the .... species they are designed for. One example is the .... put in place on fishing. By stopping people from over-fishing areas, we are .... the future supply of fish stocks. Another example is the conservation of rainforests. Many of the medicines that we use today come from .... If the rainforests are not protected, undiscovered species may become .... and we could miss out on valuable medicines.

Q2 The mountain gorilla is an **endangered** species threatened with **extinction**.

a) What is **extinction**?

....

....

b) Suggest why the **number of available habitats** might be an important factor in determining whether or not gorillas become extinct.

You don't need to know about gorillas specifically — think about how animals in general become extinct.

....

....

Q3 **Conservation programmes** are designed to protect endangered species. Explain why each of the following factors should be considered when evaluating conservation programmes:

a) interaction between species.

....

....

b) viability of populations.

....

....

Sustainable Development

Q1 a) Give a definition for the term **sustainable development**.

....

b) The human population is increasing. Give two ways in which this makes sustainable development more difficult.

1. ....

....

2. ....

....

Q2 Tick the right boxes to say whether the sentences below are **true** or **false**.

	True	False
a) Sustainable development has no impact on endangered species.	☐	☐
b) Whales still have commercial value when they are dead.	☐	☐
c) It's legal to kill whales for scientific research.	☐	☐
d) It's easy to keep track of how many whales are killed by different countries.	☐	☐
e) Scientists understand exactly how whales communicate.	☐	☐
f) Keeping whales in captivity is not useful for scientists.	☐	☐

Q3 Describe how **fishing** has changed to become more sustainable.

....

....

Q4 Explain the role that **education** can play in sustainable development.

....

....

Top Tips: Sustainable development is a hot topic. It's not just important for your exam — it's also important in the real world. Which is a pretty good reason to make sure you learn about it really.

Mixed Questions — Module B2

Q1 a) The following statements describe how **speciation** can be caused by **geographic isolation**.

Write numbers in the boxes to show the **order** the statements should be in.

☐ Different mutations create different new features in the two groups of organisms.

☐ Eventually, the two populations will change so much that they become two separate, reproductively isolated species.

☐ A physical barrier divides a population of a species, e.g. a river changes its course.

☐ Natural selection works on the features so that, if they are beneficial, they spread through each of the populations.

b) Geographic isolation can result in **small populations** with **low genetic variation**. Explain why a species with low genetic variation is at risk of **extinction**.

....

....

Q2 Read the passage below and answer the questions that follow.

> Red and grey squirrels are similar species and belong to the same genus. In Britain, red squirrels (*Sciurus vulgaris*) have become endangered because of competition from grey squirrels. Grey squirrels are generalists and are successful in different forest ecosystems. Red squirrels, on the other hand, are specialists.

a) Explain why **similar species**, like red and grey squirrels, are likely to **compete**.

....

b) Explain what is meant by the term '**generalist**'.

....

c) Fill in the missing word to complete the sentence below:

The grey squirrel's Latin name is .... *carolinensis*.

Q3 Legumes have a **mutualistic** relationship with bacteria that live in their root nodules. The bacteria turn atmospheric nitrogen into nitrogen compounds that the plants can use.

a) What name is given to these bacteria? ....

b) What do plants need nitrogen for?

....

c) Explain why the relationship between bean plants and these bacteria is **mutualistic**.

....

....

Mixed Questions — Module B2

Q4 The diagram below shows a **food chain** observed on the savannahs of Tanzania. It also shows the amount of **energy** available in each trophic level.

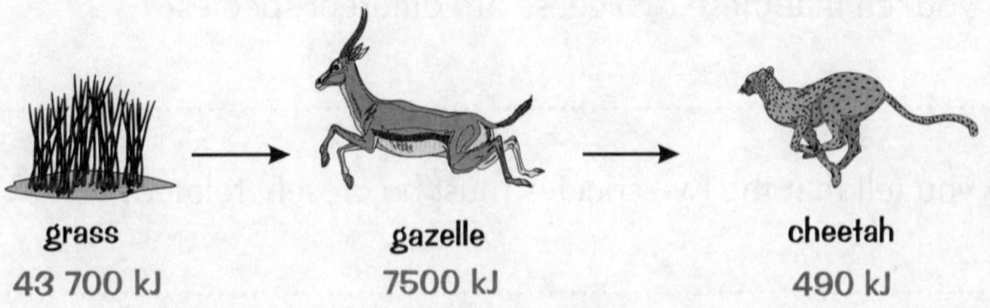

a) **i)** How much energy is lost from the 1st trophic level (grass) to the next (gazelle)?

....

ii) Calculate the efficiency of this energy transfer.

....

b) Suggest **two** ways in which energy might be lost by the gazelle.

....

....

c) Suggest how the waste products from this food chain could form the start of a new food chain.

....

....

d) **Carbon** also moves through the food chain. It is continuously being **recycled** from one form to another as the diagram below shows.

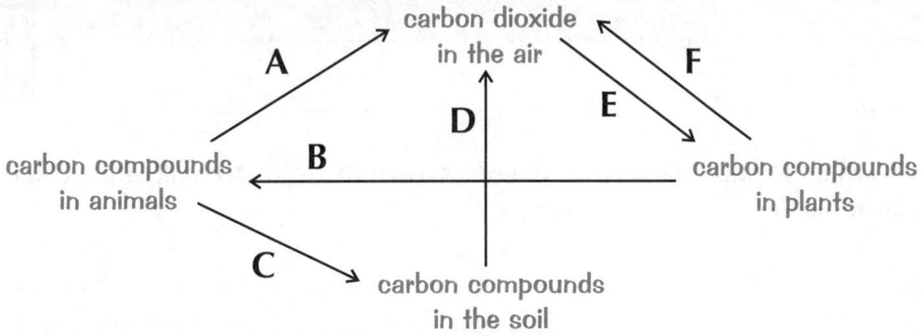

Name the processes labelled **A**, **B**, **C**, **D**, **E** and **F** in the diagram.

A .... **B** ....

C .... **D** ....

E .... **F** ....

Mixed Questions — Module B2

Q5 Two types of **goose** found in the UK are the greylag goose and the white-fronted goose. The Latin name for the greylag goose is ***Anser anser*** and the white-fronted goose is ***Anser albifrons***.

a) How can you tell that these two geese are different species?

....

b) How can you tell that the two species must be closely related?

....

c) **i)** What name is given to the system of identifying species by giving them two names?

....

ii) Explain why this system is used all over the world for naming species.

....

....

d) Explain why it's important to classify living organisms into groups such as species.

....

....

Q6 **Environmental pollution** is a major problem in some areas.

a) Magnus suspects that a paper factory down the road from his house is **polluting** a local river. Describe how Magnus could tell whether the river is polluted.

....

....

....

b) **i)** Suggest what the paper factory in Magnus's town might do to make the business more **sustainable**.

....

....

ii) Suggest how sustainable development can help **endangered species**.

....

....

....

Cells

Q1 **Bacterial cells** are different from **plant** and **animal cells**.

a) Tick the boxes to show whether the following statements apply to plant, animal or bacterial cells. Some of the statements apply to more than one type of cell.

	Bacterial Cells	Plant Cells	Animal Cells
i) A nucleus is present.	☐	☑	☑
ii) Contains a single circular strand of DNA.	☑	☐	☐
iii) DNA is arranged in chromosomes.	☐	☐	☑

b) Name two features of a typical plant cell that aren't seen in bacterial cells.

1. chloroplasts

2. vacuole

Q2 Ibrahim uses a light microscope to look at a **liver cell**. The diagram below shows what he can see.

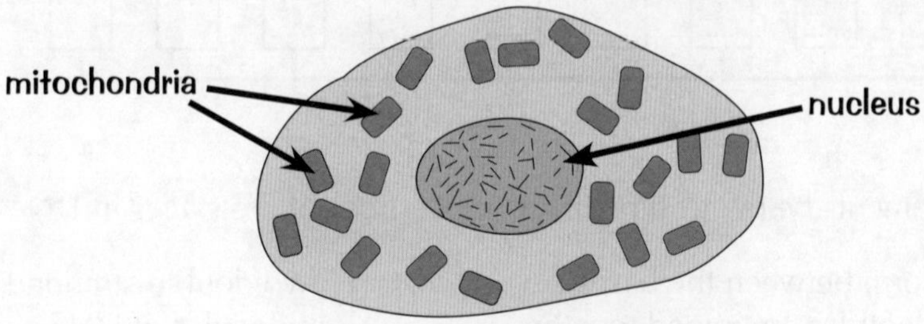

a) i) Explain why the liver cell has so many mitochondria.

Because it carries out many high energy processes

ii) Name **one** other type of cell that contains a large number of mitochondria.

muscles

b) Ibrahim uses his light microscope to look for **ribosomes** in the cell.

i) Explain why Ibrahim can't see any ribosomes.

V small

ii) In what part of the cell are ribosomes found?

cytoplasm

iii) Name the cell process which takes place at the ribosomes.

respiration reactions.

DNA

Q1 Choose from the words below to complete the passage about the **structure** of **DNA**.

U	bases	A	helix	chromosomes	
protein	G	B	cross	genes	complementary

chromosomes are long, coiled molecules of DNA divided into short sections called genes . DNA is a double-stranded helix made up of four different bases — these are G, C, A and T. The two DNA strands are joined together by cross links, which form between complement base-pairs.

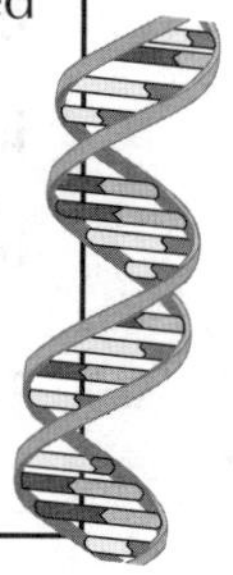

Q2 Complete the diagram below to show which **bases** will form the complementary strand of DNA.

A	C	T	G	C	A	A	T	G
T	G	A	C	G	T	T	A	C

Q3 Number the statements below to show the correct order of the stages in **DNA replication**.

☐ Cross links form between the bases and the nucleotides are joined together.

☐ Two double-stranded molecules of DNA are formed.

☐ The DNA double helix 'unzips' to form two single strands.

☐ Bases on free-floating nucleotides pair up with complementary bases on the DNA.

Q4 A **model** of **DNA** was first developed by two scientists called Watson and Crick. They used data that had been collected by other scientists.

a) **i)** Tick the box next to the statement below that correctly describes some of the data they used.

1. X-ray data showing there was a single chain of DNA wound in a helix. ☐
2. X-ray data showing there were two chains of DNA wound in a helix. ☐
3. Infra-red data showing there were two chains of DNA wound in a helix. ☐

ii) What other data did Watson and Crick use to develop their model?

....

b) Suggest why new discoveries like Watson and Crick's are not always immediately accepted.

Big idea
now.

Protein Synthesis

Q1 Circle the correct words in the pairs to complete the sentences below.

a) A gene is a section of DNA that codes for a **particular protein / cell structure**.

b) Each gene contains **a different / the same** sequence of bases.

c) Proteins are made up of chains of **amino acids / glucose**.

d) Each amino acid is coded for by a sequence of **three / four** bases.

Q2 Choose from the words below to complete the passage about **cell function**.

on	**full set**	**off**	**enzymes**
functions	**divides**	**amino acids**	

The proteins produced by a cell determine how it functions . For example, cell reactions are controlled by proteins called enzymes . Every cell contains a full set of genes, but some of these genes are switched off — this means that the proteins they code for can't be made. As a result, only the genes that are switched on determine the function of the cell.

Q3 DNA controls the production of **proteins**.

a) How do **amino acids** determine the function of a protein?

....

b) How is the **sequence** of amino acids determined?

....

Q4 **mRNA** is a copy of the code in DNA.

a) Describe the role of mRNA in the production of proteins.

....

....

b) Explain why a **copy** of the DNA code is needed to make proteins.

....

....

Functions of Proteins

Q1 Draw lines to match each **protein** to its type and function.

protein	type	function
insulin	structural protein	transports oxygen around the body
haemoglobin	hormone	strengthens connective tissues
collagen	carrier molecule	regulates blood sugar level

Q2 a) Tick the boxes to show whether the sentences are **true** or **false**.

	True	False
i) Enzymes slow down chemical reactions in living cells.	☐	☐
ii) The reactions involved in photosynthesis are controlled by enzymes.	☐	☐
iii) Enzymes don't control reactions involved with protein synthesis.	☐	☐

b) Write a correct version of each false sentence in the space below.

....

....

Q3 Enzymes are **biological catalysts**. They have a **high specificity** for their substrate.

a) What is a **catalyst**?

....

b) i) What does it mean when enzymes are described as having '**high specificity**'?

....

ii) Explain why enzymes have a high specificity for their substrate using the term '**lock and key mechanism**'.

....

....

c) In the space provided, draw a labelled diagram to show how an enzyme's shape allows it to break substances down.

More on Enzymes

Q1 This graph shows the results from an investigation into the effect of **temperature** on the rate of an **enzyme-catalysed** reaction.

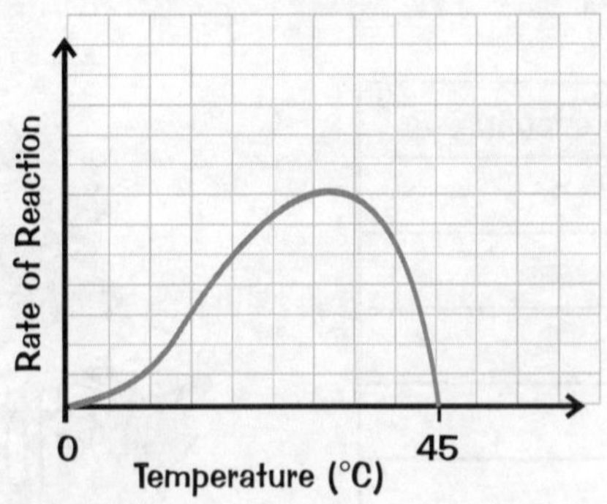

a) What is the **optimum** temperature for this enzyme?

....

b) Explain why the rate of an enzyme-catalysed reaction is **slow** at **low temperatures**.

....

....

c) Describe what happens to an enzyme at temperatures **above** its optimum and give the technical term for this.

....

....

Q2 Professor Cuten wants to calculate the $\mathbf{Q_{10}}$ value of an enzyme-catalysed reaction. The **rate of reaction** at different temperatures is shown in the table below.

Temperature (°C)	Rate of Reaction (cm^3/s)
10	2
20	6
30	18
40	54
50	162

a) What does a Q_{10} value show?

....

....

$$Q_{10} = \frac{\text{rate at higher temperature}}{\text{rate at lower temperature}}$$

b) i) Using the formula in the box above calculate the Q_{10} value of the reaction.

....

ii) What does this Q_{10} value tell you about the rate of the reaction?

....

More on Enzymes

Q3 Stuart has a sample of an enzyme and he is trying to find out what its **optimum pH** is. Stuart tests the enzyme by **timing** how long it takes to break down a substance at different pH levels. The results of Stuart's experiment are shown in the table below.

pH	time taken for reaction in seconds
2	101
4	83
6	17
8	76
10	99
12	102

a) On the grid below draw a line graph of the results of the experiment.

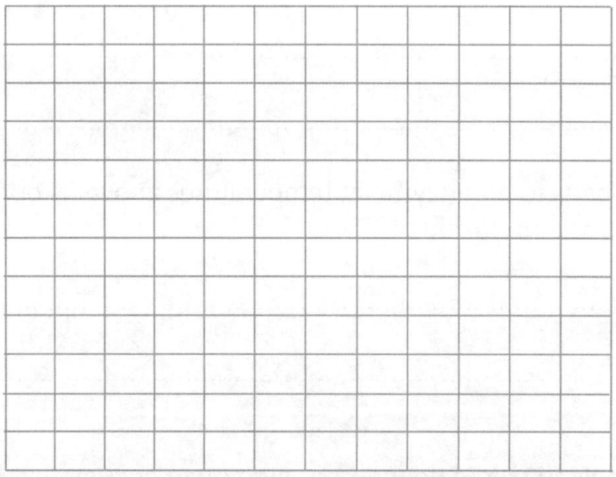

b) What is the **optimum** pH for the enzyme?

c) Explain why the reaction is very slow at certain pH levels.

d) Would you expect to find this enzyme in the stomach? Explain your answer.

Remember, the pH in the stomach is very low.

e) Describe **two** things that Stuart could do to make sure his experiment is a fair test.

1.

2.

Mutations

Q1 a) Tick the correct boxes to show whether the following statements are **true** or **false**.

	True	False
i) Mutations are always harmful.		
ii) Mutations can occur spontaneously.		
iii) Mutations can prevent the production of a protein.		
iv) Mutations never lead to the production of different proteins.		
v) Mutations are changes to the cell cytoplasm.		
vi) Mutations sometimes have no effect.		

Ben's pet ant had been mute since the unfortunate squishing incident.

b) Write a correct version of each false sentence in the space below.

....

....

....

Q2 Suggest explanations for the following facts.

a) In 1986, a nuclear reactor at Chernobyl in the Ukraine exploded. Afterwards, the rate of thyroid cancer amongst children in the surrounding region increased by approximately 1000%.

....

....

b) Smokers are more likely to suffer from lung cancer than non-smokers.

....

....

Q3 Suggest how some mutations might be **beneficial**.

....

....

....

Top Tips: Sadly mutations in the real world are nowhere near as awesome as the ones in films and comics — no mutation has ever given anyone x-ray vision, telepathy or the ability to fly. Make sure you know how mutations are caused and the sorts of results they really have.

Multiplying Cells

Q1 Mitosis is a type of cell division.

What does mitosis produce cells for?

....

....

Q2 Complete the passage using the words provided below.

divide	centre	replicated	opposite	line up

Before mitosis starts, the DNA in a cell is ....

At the beginning of mitosis, the DNA coils into double-armed chromosomes that .... along the .... of the cell.

The chromosomes then .... as the cell fibres pull them apart.

The two arms of each chromosome move to .... poles of the cell.

Q3 Many creatures have evolved to be **multicellular**.

a) Explain two advantages of being **multicellular** compared to being **single-celled**.

1. ....

....

2. ....

....

b) Suggest why multicellular organisms need the following specialised organ systems:

i) a nervous system

....

ii) a respiratory system

....

iii) a circulatory system

....

Meiosis, Gametes and Fertilisation

Q1 Choose from the following words to complete the passage below.

haploid	meiosis	sperm	two copies	mitosis
cytoplasm	one copy	diploid	egg	

Gametes are the .... and .... cells. They're formed by a process called .... In mammals, all body cells are ...., which means they contain .... of each chromosome. However, gametes are ...., which means they contain .... of each chromosome.

Q2 Tick the boxes to show whether the following statements are **true** or **false**.

	True	False
a) Fertilisation reduces genetic variation.	☐	☐
b) At fertilisation gametes combine to form a haploid zygote.	☐	☐
c) Genes on the chromosomes combine to control the characteristics of the zygote.	☐	☐

Q3 a) Describe what happens in:

i) The **first** meiotic division.

....

ii) The **second** meiotic division.

....

b) Explain how this produces cells that are genetically different.

....

....

Q4 **Sperm** are adapted to fertilising egg cells. Suggest how the following features make sperm cells adapted to their function:

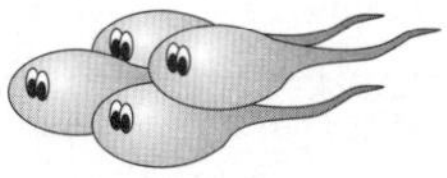

a) many mitochondria.

....

b) an acrosome.

....

Stem Cells, Differentiation and Growth

Q1 Tick the box next to the correct definition of **stem cells**.

1. Cells found only in embryos. ☐
2. Cells in plants that form the tissues within stems. ☐
3. Undifferentiated cells that can develop into different types of cells, tissues and organs. ☐
4. Undifferentiated cells that develop into a particular type of cell, tissue or organ. ☐

Q2 Give three differences in the **growth** of plants and animals.

1. ....

2. ....

3. ....

Q3 In the future, **embryonic stem cells** might be used to replace faulty cells in sick people.

a) How are **embryonic** stem cells different from **adult** stem cells?

....

....

b) Suggest one way in which embryonic stem cells could be used to treat a medical condition.

....

....

Q4 People have **different opinions** when it comes to **stem cell research**.

a) Give one argument **in favour** of stem cell research.

....

....

b) Give one argument **against** stem cell research.

....

....

Growth

Q1 Keeley wants to measure the growth of her pet batpig.

a) Suggest one **advantage** of measuring the batpig's growth using:

i) length ......not representative......

ii) wet mass ......fluctuates......

iii) dry mass ......dead......

b) Suggest one **disadvantage** of measuring the batpig's growth using only:

i) length ......Easy......

ii) wet mass ......Easy......

iii) dry mass ......Accurate......

c) Which of the methods above is the best way of measuring growth?

......Dry......

Q2 The graph on the right is an example of a **human growth curve**. It shows three different phases of growth.

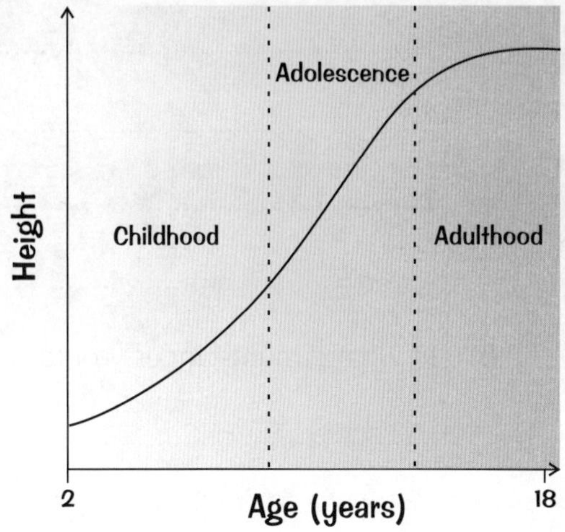

a) Describe the trend in growth shown during **childhood**.

......rapid......

......steady......

b) **i)** During which phase on this growth curve is growth **fastest**?

......adolescence......

ii) Name another phase of **rapid human growth**, which is not shown on this growth curve.

......old age......

Q3 Different parts of an organism grow at **different rates**. Give one example of this and explain the reason behind it.

......Head......

......need a good brain......

....

Respiration

Q1 **Respiration** happens in every cell in your body.

a) Complete the **chemical equation** below for **aerobic respiration**:

$C_6H_{12}O_6$ + $6O_2$ → $6CO_2$ + $6H_2O$ (+ energy)

b) Circle the correct word in each pair below to complete the sentences.

i) The energy released by respiration is used to **break down** / **make** a small molecule called **ATM** / **ATP**.

ii) This molecule is the source of **oxygen** / **energy** for lots of cell reactions.

c) Explain why the rate of respiration is affected by temperature and pH.

....

....

Q2 Humans can respire **aerobically** or **anaerobically**.

a) Give two disadvantages of **anaerobic** respiration compared to aerobic respiration.

1. Less effective

....

2. Latic acid

....

b) In what circumstances would someone use anaerobic respiration?

Lack of O_2

excercise

c) Write the **word equation** for anaerobic respiration in humans.

glucose → latic acid (+ energy)

Top Tips: If you want to nail the respiration questions in the exam, make sure you know the difference between aerobic and anaerobic respiration — aerobic is with oxygen, anaerobic is without. And it's the presence or absence of oxygen that causes different products to be made.

Respiration

Q3 Judy decided to measure the **respiratory quotient** of two mice. Her data is presented in the table below.

	Oxygen Used (cm^3)	Carbon Dioxide Produced (cm^3)
Mouse A	**26.5**	**31.8**
Mouse B	**29.1**	**26.2**

$$RQ = \frac{\text{Amount of } CO_2 \text{ produced}}{\text{Amount of } O_2 \text{ used}}$$

Calculate the respiratory quotient of each mouse using the formula given above.

a) Mouse A: ....

b) Mouse B: ....

Q4 Jim takes part in a race. The **graph** below shows Jim's **oxygen consumption** before, during and after the race.

a) **i)** Describe what happens to Jim's oxygen consumption **during** and **after** the race.

gradually reduces

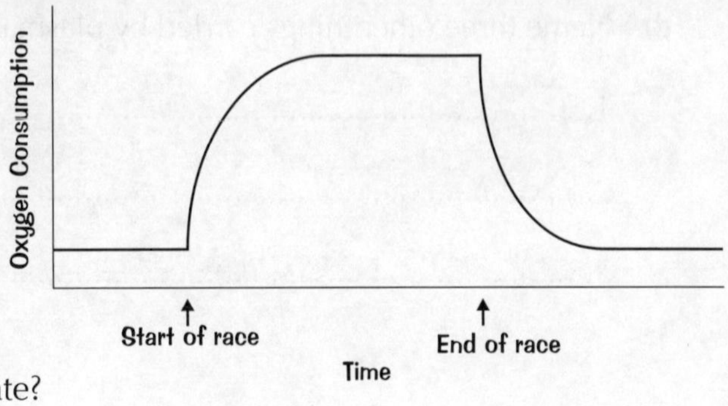

ii) What does this show about his respiration rate?

fast

iii) What can Jim's rate of oxygen consumption be used to estimate?

Lung capacity

b) Jim's leg muscles are painful after the race. Suggest what substance caused the pain.

Latic acid

c) Why does Jim's **breathing rate** not return to normal immediately after the race?

O_2 debt

d) Why does Jim's **heart rate** not return to normal immediately after the race?

....

Functions of the Blood

Q1 **Plasma** carries just about everything around the body.

a) What is plasma?

liquid blood

b) Which of the following is a **digested food product** carried by plasma? Circle the correct answer.

starch **protein** **glucose** **oxygen**

c) i) Suggest one **waste product** carried by plasma.

urea

ii) Where is this waste product carried from and to?

blood to kidneys

d) Name three other things carried by plasma.

1. platelets CO_2
2. hormones
3. antibodies

Q2 Use the words below to complete the passage about the structure of **red blood cells**.

Some words can be used more than once.

body tissues	**large**	**biconcave**	**small**	**nucleus**
carbon dioxide	**oxygen**	**capillaries**	**haemoglobin**	**oxyhaemoglobin**

Red blood cells are biconcave in shape, which means they have a large surface area to volume ratio for absorbing oxygen. They have no nucleus, but their cytoplasm is full of O_2, which combines with haemoglobin in the lungs to form oxyhaemo- . In capillaries, the reverse of this reaction happens to release oxygen to the cells. Red blood cells are very flexible, which means that they can fit easily through the capillaries.

Blood Vessels

Q1 Draw lines to match each of the words below with its correct description.

vein	vessel involved in the exchange of materials at the tissues
valve	vessel that takes blood away from the heart
artery	keeps the blood flowing in the right direction
lumen	vessel that takes blood to the heart
capillary	hole in the middle of a tube

Q2 Circle the correct word in each of the sentences below.

a) **Arteries** / **Veins** contain valves to prevent the blood going backwards.

b) **Capillaries** / **Veins** have walls that are permeable.

c) **Veins** / **Arteries** have walls that are thick and muscular.

d) The blood pressure in the **arteries** / **veins** is higher than in the **arteries** / **veins**.

Q3 Two blood vessels are dissected from a piece of meat. One is a **vein** and the other is an **artery**. Measurements taken from both vessels are shown in the table below.

	Thickness of wall (mm)	Diameter of lumen (mm)
Blood vessel A	1.2	3.9
Blood vessel B	0.5	5.2

a) i) Which blood vessel would you expect to be the **vein**? Explain your answer.

vein

ii) Suggest one way you could confirm this.

check for valves

b) When tested, one of the blood vessels was found to be much more **elastic** than the other. Which one would you expect this to be? Explain your answer.

B LOSS MUSCULAR

The Heart

Q1 The diagram below shows the human **heart**, as seen from the front.
The left atrium has been labelled. Complete the remaining labels **a)** to **j)**.

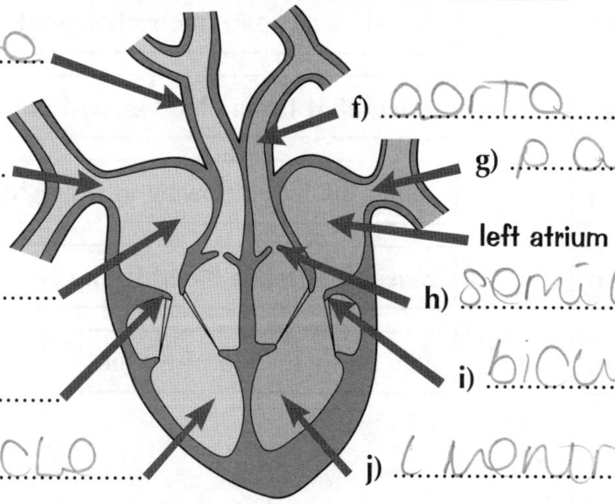

a) veno cava

b) p vein / aorta

c) r atrium

d) tricuspid

e) r venticle

f) aorta

g) p artery

h) semilunar

i) bicuspid

j) L ventricle

Q2 Mammals have a **double circulatory system** in which blood is pumped by the heart.

a) What is a double circulatory system?

2 heart sides

b) Explain why having a double circulatory system is an advantage for mammals

....

....

....

Q3 Valves are present in the left and right ventricles of the heart.

a) What is the function of the heart valves?

stop backflow

b) Describe the function of the ventricles.

pump blood

c) Explain why the wall of the left ventricle is thicker than the wall of the right ventricle.

pump to whole body

....

Top Tips: When doctors use a stethoscope to listen to your heart, it's actually the valves closing that they hear. Make sure you understand why there are valves in the heart and veins.

Selective Breeding

Q1 Garfield wants to selectively breed one type of plant for its **fruit**, and another as an **ornamental house plant**.

a) What is selective breeding?

....

....

b) Suggest **two** characteristics that Garfield could select for in each kind of plant.

Fruit plant: ....

Ornamental house plant: ....

Q2 Describe two long term **disadvantages** of selective breeding.

1. Small gene pool

....

2. inethical

....

Q3 Many breeds of **domesticated dog** have been bred for their **friendly temperament**.

a) Describe how selective breeding from an **aggressive** wolf-like stock of dogs could produce a breed with a more **friendly** temperament.

....

....

....

b) Explain why some domesticated dog breeds are likely to suffer from genetic disorders.

....

....

....

Genetic Engineering

Q1 **Genetic engineering** has produced a range of useful products.

a) Put the following stages of genetic engineering in order by numbering them 1–4.

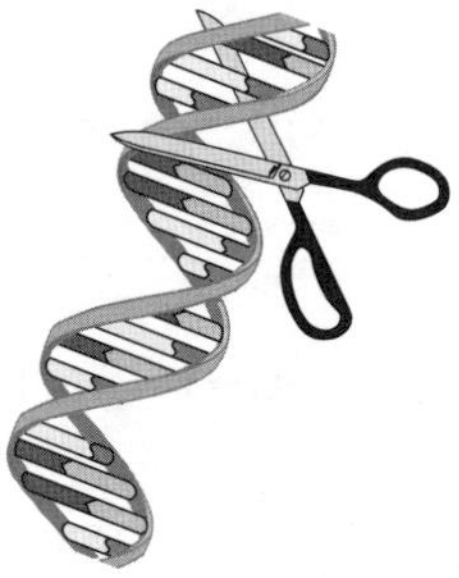

[3] The gene is inserted into the DNA of another organism.

[2] The gene is cut from the DNA and isolated.

[4] The organism replicates.

[1] The gene for the characteristic is selected.

b) **i)** Suggest one **advantage** of genetic engineering.

desired characteristic

ii) Suggest one **risk** of genetic engineering.

can harm

c) Describe one example of genetic engineering involving bacteria.

insulin

Q2 Plants can be genetically engineered.

a) Describe how genetic engineering can be used in **rice** to prevent Vitamin A deficiency.

golden rice

put beta carotene in rice plant

b) Suggest how genetic engineering could improve crop yield.

antifreeze gene

Q3 Some people are **worried** about the ethical issues involved in genetic engineering.

a) Explain why this is.

unknown

b) Do you think that scientists should be carrying out genetic engineering? Explain your answer.

yes

food to cope w/ population

Gene Therapy and Cloning Animals

Q1 **Dolly** the sheep was cloned from an adult cell.

a) What are clones?

genetic copies

b) Name the **method** of cloning used to produce Dolly.

nuclour transfer

c) Write the correct letter (A, B, C or D) in the box next to each stage below to show where it belongs on the diagram.

A nucleus is removed from a sheep's egg cell. 1

The embryo is implanted in the uterus of a surrogate mother sheep. 4

A nucleus from an udder cell of a different sheep is inserted into the egg cell. 2

The egg cell is given an electric shock to make it start dividing. 3

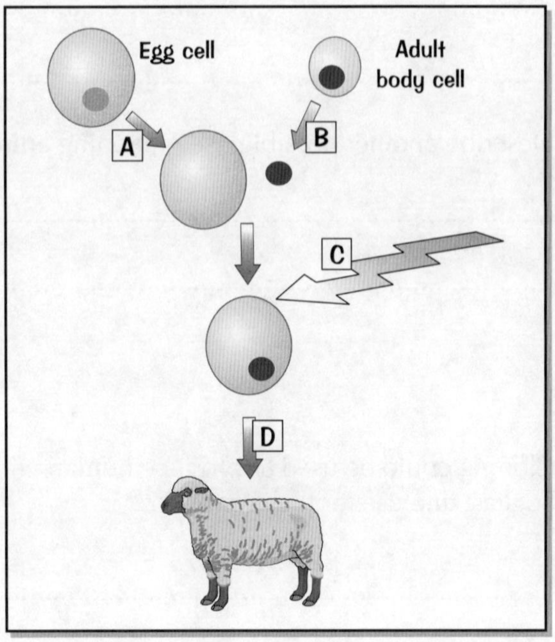

Q2 In the future it might be possible to treat some health disorders using **gene therapy**.

a) What is gene therapy?

Altering genes of foetus

b) Tick the box next to the statement which is **true**.

Gene therapy can only be used to alter the genes of body cells. ☐

Gene therapy can only be used to alter the genes of gametes. ☐

Gene therapy can be used to alter the genes of gametes or body cells. ☑

c) Explain why gene therapy involving gametes is controversial.

designing a child

Uses and Risks of Cloning Animals

Q1 Some **animals** could be genetically engineered to have **organs** suitable for transplantation into humans.

a) Describe the possible use of **cloning** in producing these organs.

organs are identical to mother

b) Describe **two risks** involved with cloning animals.

Mutations
Susceptable to disease

c) Describe another possible use of cloning animals.

food

Q2 Cloning could be used to produce **human** embryos. Suggest **one** use for these embryos.

stem cell research

Q3 Summarise the **ethical** issues involved in cloning humans.

Play god
reduced life expectancy

Top Tips: Hmmm, cloning. It's always in the news, with various mad scientists regularly claiming to have produced the first human clone. You have to take this type of story with a pinch of salt though, because the media often aren't too keen on letting the facts get in the way of a good story.

Cloning Plants

Q1 Plants are often grown commercially using **tissue culture**.

a) Number the boxes below to put the stages of tissue culture in the correct order.

[3] The tissue is grown in a growth medium under aseptic conditions.

[2] Several small pieces of tissue are removed from the parent plant.

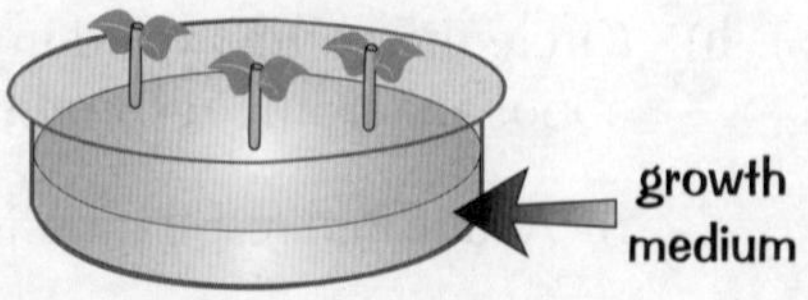

[4] When the tissues produce shoots and roots they're moved to potting compost to carry on growing.

[1] A plant with the desired characteristics is chosen.

b) Suggest two substances that are needed in the growth medium.

1. gl carbon dioxide 2. oxygen

c) Why is the tissue grown under aseptic conditions?

prevent disease

Q2 Explain why cloning plant cells is easier than cloning animal cells.

cells can differentiate

Q3 Alfie is setting up a banana farm and is trying to decide whether or not to use **cloned** plants.

a) Suggest two **advantages** of using cloned plants.

1. Desired

2. identical

b) Suggest two **disadvantages** of using cloned plants.

1. expensive

2. susceptable

Mixed Questions — Module B3

Q1 Humans can respire **aerobically** and **anaerobically**.

a) Give a definition of respiration, including where it happens in the body.

enorgy from glucose

b) Circle the correct word in each pair to complete the following sentences about **anaerobic respiration** in humans.

i) Anaerobic respiration is respiration without **glucose** / **oxygen**.

ii) The incomplete breakdown of glucose during anaerobic respiration produces **lactic acid** / **water**.

iii) **Less** / **More** energy is released per glucose molecule during anaerobic respiration than during aerobic respiration.

c) Explain why anaerobic respiration leads to an **oxygen debt**.

Not enough oxygen
latic acid break dawn needs O_2

Q2 **Plants** and **animals** grow in different ways.

a) Describe how plant growth differs from animal growth regarding:

i) cell enlargement

plant cells elongate

ii) cell division

iii) cell differentiation

plants can always differentate

b) The growth of both plants and animals can be measured by recording how their **wet mass** increases over time. Give one **disadvantage** of this.

Includes water, so can fluctuate

Mixed Questions — Module B3

Q3 a) What unique characteristic do **embryonic stem cells** have which adult stem cells don't have?

undifferentiated

b) Scientists have experimented with growing stem cells in different conditions.
What is the name of the process by which stem cells **divide** for growth?

miosis

c) Suggest why scientists are especially interested in **embryonic** stem cells.

curing illness

d) Some people disagree with stem cell research on ethical grounds.
Describe one **ethical issue** surrounding stem cell research.

Playing God
Human being

Q4 The diagram shows part of the **circulatory system**.

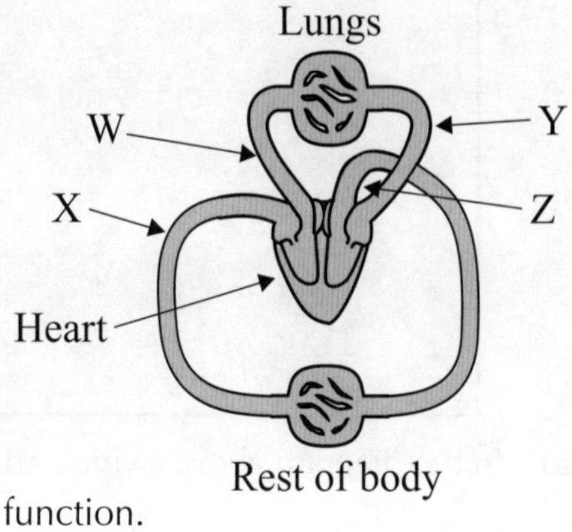

a) Name the blood vessels labelled W, X, Y and Z.

W vena cava

X pulmonary artery vein

Y p artery

Z aorta

b) i) Explain how the structure of an artery is adapted for its function.

thick cell wall

ii) Explain how the structure of a capillary is adapted for its function.

1 cell thick

c) i) Which type of blood vessel contains valves?

vein

ii) What is the function of these valves?

control flow no backflow

Mixed Questions — Module B3

Q5 The sequence of bases in part of one strand of a **DNA** molecule is as follows:

A–A–T–C–C–A–A–T–C

a) Write down the **complementary sequence** of bases on the other strand of DNA.

A + T , C + G

b) Describe the relationship between DNA and proteins.

DNA is made up of protein

Q6 "Dolly the sheep" was produced in 1997 in Edinburgh, and was the world's first clone of an adult mammal. The diagram illustrates the process by which clones like Dolly can be produced.

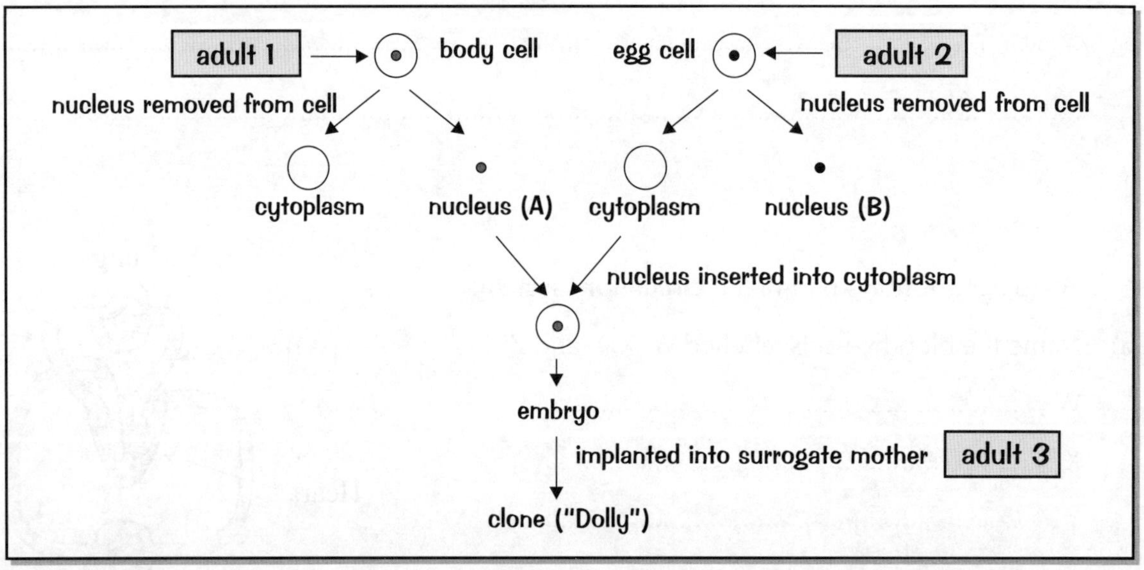

a) In the diagram above, which adult (1, 2 or 3) will the clone be identical to, and why?

1 and 3 because DNA is in nucleus

b) An unfertilised sheep's egg contains 27 chromosomes. How many chromosomes will there be in:

i) the nucleus labelled A: 27

ii) the nucleus labelled B: 27/2

iii) the cloned sheep's body cells: 27

c) Suggest a potential benefit of cloning animals.

carry forward desired genes

Estimating Population Sizes

Q1 Some students wanted to estimate the size of the **population of clover plants** around their school.

a) Explain the difference between a population and a community.

....

....

b) The school field is 250 m long by 180 m wide. Hannah counted 11 clover plants in a 1 m^2 area of the field. Approximately how many clover plants are there likely to be on the whole field?

....

c) Lisa decided to collect data from five different 1 m^2 areas of the school field. Her results are shown in the table below.

	Area 1	Area 2	Area 3	Area 4	Area 5
No. of plants	11	9	8	9	7

i) What was the **average** number of clover plants per m^2 in Lisa's survey?

....

ii) Use Lisa's data to estimate the population size of clover plants on the field.

....

d) Whose estimation of population size is likely to be more accurate? Explain your answer.

....

Q2 In a capture-recapture experiment, there were **30** animals in both the first and second samples. **Seven** of the animals in the second sample were marked.

a) Estimate the population size using the formula in the box below.

$$\text{Population Size} = \frac{\text{number in first sample} \times \text{number in second sample}}{\text{number in second sample previously marked}}$$

....

....

b) Give three **assumptions** that you have to make when you're using capture-recapture data to estimate population size.

1. ....

2. ....

3. ....

Ecosystems and Distribution of Organisms

Q1 a) Circle the correct definition of the word '**ecosystem**' from the choices below.

The place where an organism lives.

All the organisms living in a particular area.

All the organisms living in a particular area, as well as all the non-living (abiotic) conditions.

b) Explain the difference between a **habitat** and an **ecosystem**.

....

....

c) Ecosystems are often described as being '**self-supporting**' apart from their energy source. Explain what this means.

....

....

Q2 a) Taylor is studying the **distribution** of two species of moss across the school playground. Describe how he could carry out a **transect** with **quadrats** to help with his investigation.

....

....

Taylor draws the following **kite diagram** from the results of his transect:

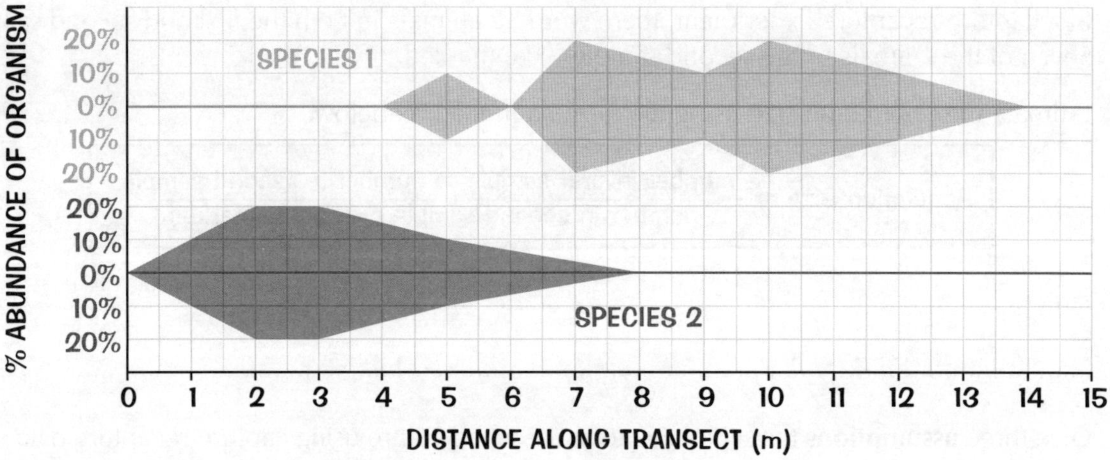

b) Describe the distribution of **species 2** along the transect.

....

....

Zonation

Q1 The distribution of organisms can be affected by **abiotic factors**.

a) Explain what is meant by the term '**abiotic factors**'.

....

b) List **three** abiotic factors that could affect the distribution of an organism.

....

....

Q2 Molly is doing a science project on **zonation** along the coastline near her town.

a) Explain what is meant by the term '**zonation**'.

....

b) Molly draws a sketch of what she finds on one particular section of the shore and marks on some observations about the abiotic conditions at the bottom.

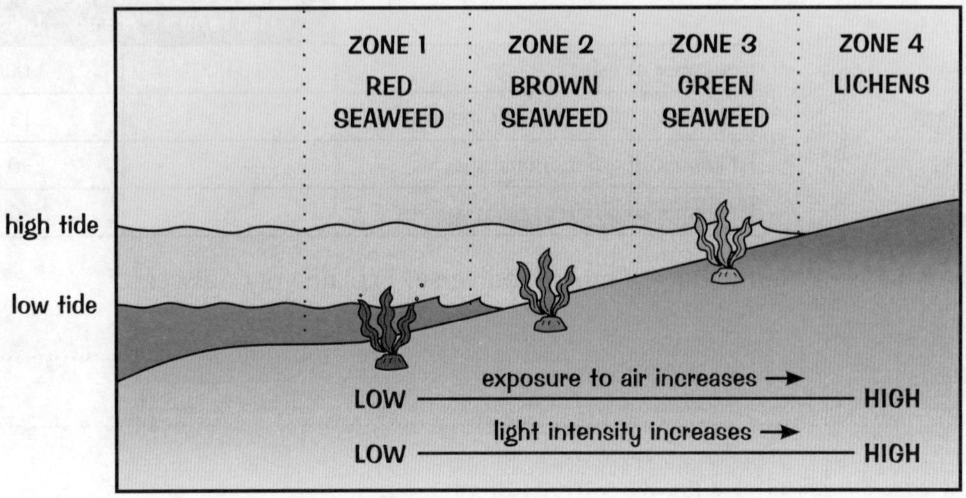

i) Which organism from the diagram would you expect to be **least tolerant** to low light intensity? Explain your answer.

....

....

ii) Using Molly's sketch and her observations about light intensity and exposure to air, suggest why there is more **brown seaweed** in zone 2 than in zone 1.

....

....

Top Tips: If you get a zonation question in the exam, don't panic. Just remember to think about the abiotic factors involved and how they might affect where different organisms are found.

Biodiversity

Q1 What is '**biodiversity**' a measure of? Underline **three** correct statements from the list below.

The number of different species in an area.

The variation in abiotic factors in an area.

The number of different habitats in an area.

The amount of variation between individuals of the same species in an area.

The number of individuals of one species in an area.

Q2 Fish farms are **artificial ecosystems**.

a) What is the key difference between a natural ecosystem and an artificial ecosystem?

....

....

The table below shows data for a fish farm and a natural lake.

	Fish Farm	Lake
Number of fish	10 000	3 000
Number of different fish species	1	15
Number of other animal species	3	50
Number of different plant species	10	50

b) Which of the ecosystems above is **more biodiverse**? Explain your answer.

....

....

c) Suggest why the **lake** has a greater variety of:

i) animal species ....

....

ii) plant species ....

....

Q3 Explain why **forestry plantations** are less biodiverse than **natural woodlands**.

....

....

....

Photosynthesis

Q1 Complete the chemical equation for photosynthesis.

$6CO_2$ + ... $\xrightarrow[\text{chlorophyll}]{\text{LIGHT}}$ $C_6H_{12}O_6$ + ...

Q2 Complete the sentences below by circling the correct word(s) from each pair.

a) Photosynthesis is a **three** / **two** stage process.

b) Photosynthesis takes place in the **chloroplasts** / **nucleus** of plant cells.

c) First, light energy is used to split **water** / **carbon dioxide** into oxygen gas and hydrogen ions.

d) Then **oxygen gas** / **carbon dioxide gas** combines with the hydrogen ions to make glucose and water.

Q3 New potato plants are grown from potato **tubers**, which contain stores of **insoluble starch**.

a) Suggest how the new plants obtain the energy needed for growth.

....

b) Suggest why the plants no longer need this energy source once they have grown above the soil.

....

c) Give **two** reasons why the tubers store glucose as **insoluble starch**.

....

....

Q4 Complete the passage about **glucose** by choosing the correct words from the list below.

proteins	lipids	walls	convert	leaves	energy	cellulose

Plants make glucose in their .... Some of it is used for respiration, which releases .... and allows the plant to .... the rest of the glucose into other substances. In rapidly growing plants, glucose is converted into .... to build cell ....
Some glucose is combined with nitrates from the soil to make amino acids and ...., which are used for growth and repair. Glucose can also be turned into .... for storage in seeds.

Understanding Photosynthesis

Q1 Scientists have been studying plant growth for centuries.

Describe the view of **early Greek scientists** on how plants grow and gain mass.

....

....

Q2 In the 1600s **Jan van Helmont** carried out an experiment to investigate how plants gain mass. He planted a willow tree in some soil and left it for 5 years, adding only water to the soil.

a) Describe the results of van Helmont's experiment.

....

....

b) What conclusion did van Helmont draw from these results?

....

c) Explain how van Helmont's experiment helped our understanding of photosynthesis.

....

....

Q3 Miss Webb's biology class are recreating some of **Joseph Priestley's** famous experiments.

a) They place a lit candle in a sealed container and leave it until it goes out. Describe what you would expect to happen when they try to re-light the candle in the sealed container.

....

b) The class carry out the experiment again. This time they place a green plant in the container along with the candle. Describe what you would expect to happen when they try to re-light the candle in a week's time.

....

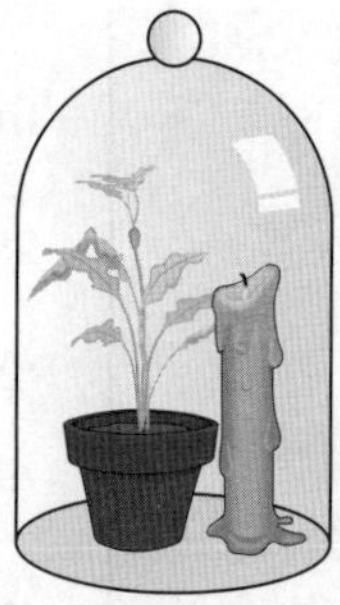

c) Explain your answer to part **b)**.

....

....

More on Photosynthesis

Q1 Below are some straightforward questions about **limiting factors**.

a) List **three** factors that can limit the rate of photosynthesis.

....

....

b) Explain the meaning of the term "limiting factor".

....

Q2 Jacquie was growing some herbs in her kitchen. Changes taking place in her kitchen that affect the rate of photosynthesis are shown in the table below.

Change in conditions	Environmental factor(s) changed	Effect on photosynthesis
A cooling fan is turned on.		
More plants are added to the room.		
Jacquie's family enter the room.		
An electric heater is switched on.		
A light bulb is switched on.		
The blinds are closed and lights switched off.		

a) For each statement, identify which environmental factor (or factors) will have changed — **carbon dioxide**, **temperature** or **light**. Write your answers in the table.

b) Predict the effect of each change on the rate of photosynthesis by choosing from **increase, decrease** or **no effect.** Write your answers in the table.

Q3 Describe how scientists used **isotopes** to work out whether the **oxygen** produced in photosynthesis came from carbon dioxide or water.

....

....

....

More on Photosynthesis

Q4 Richard grows house plants **commercially** for sale to garden centres. Over the years Richard has spent a lot of money building **glasshouses** in which to grow his plants.

a) Richard **burns fuel** in his glasshouses to increase the air temperature, making his plants grow faster. Burning the fuel also releases carbon dioxide.

i) Describe the effect of increasing the air temperature on the rate of photosynthesis.

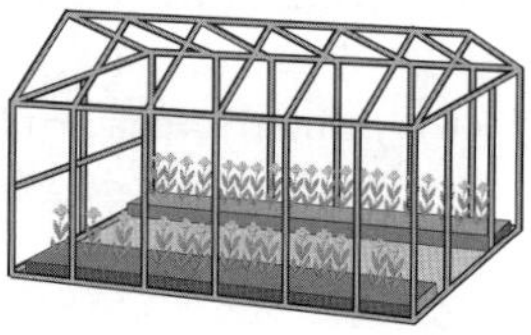

ii) Suggest why the carbon dioxide released by the fuel makes the plants **grow faster**.

b) Richard's glasshouses also have **artificial lighting**.

i) **When** would Richard use the artificial lighting?

ii) Suggest a **benefit** of providing artificial lighting.

Q5 Average daytime summer temperatures in different habitats are recorded in the table below.

Area of the world	Temperature (°C)
Forest	19
Arctic	0
Desert	32
Grassland	22
Rainforest	27

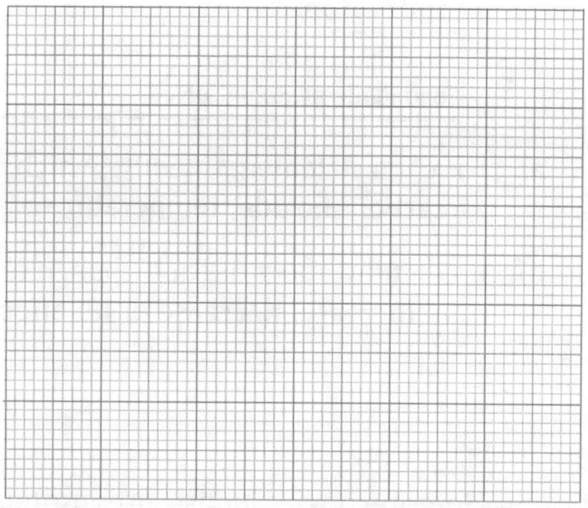

a) Plot a **bar chart** for these results on the grid.

b) From the values for temperature, in which area would you expect fewest plants to grow?

c) Suggest a reason for your answer.

Diffusion

Q1 Complete the passage below by circling the correct word in each pair.

Diffusion is the **direct / net** movement of particles from an area of **higher / lower** concentration to an area of **higher / lower** concentration. It's caused by the **uniform / random** movement of individual particles. The rate of diffusion is faster when the concentration gradient is **bigger / smaller**. It is slower when there is a **large / small** distance over which diffusion occurs and when there is **more / less** surface area for diffusion to take place across.

Q2 The first diagram below shows a **cup of water** which has just had a **drop of dye** added.

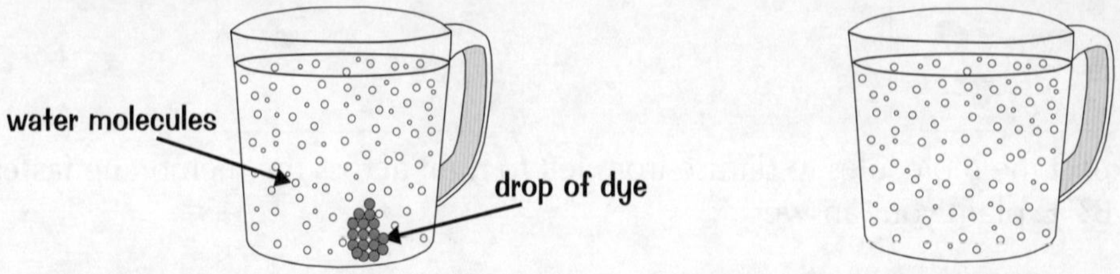

a) In the second cup above, draw the molecules of **dye** in the water after an hour.

b) Predict how the rate of diffusion of the dye would change if a large drop of dye was used rather than a small drop of dye.

....

c) Explain the movement of the dye molecules in terms of differences in concentration.

....

....

Q3 Patsy was studying in her bedroom. Her dad was cooking curry for tea in the kitchen. Soon Patsy could smell the curry that her dad was making.

a) Her dad was warm so he switched on a fan. Suggest what effect the fan would have on the rate that the curry particles spread through the house.

....

b) After tasting the curry, Patsy's dad added more curry powder. What effect would this have on the smell of the curry? Explain your answer using the word **concentration**.

....

....

Diffusion

Q4 Some statements about **diffusion** are written below.
Decide which are correct and then write **true** or **false** in the spaces.

a) Diffusion takes place in all types of substances. ....

b) Large protein molecules can diffuse across cell membranes. ....

c) Diffusion happens more quickly when there is a higher concentration gradient. ....

d) A larger surface area makes diffusion happen more quickly. ....

e) When there is a larger distance for particles to travel across, the rate of diffusion is faster. ....

Q5 Two diagrams of diffusion are shown below.

A

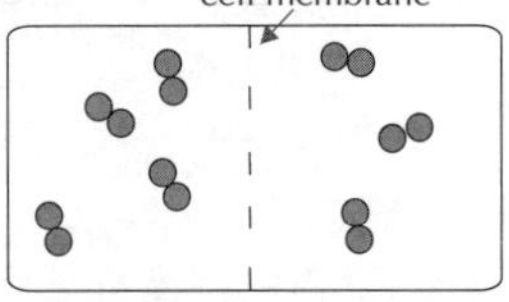

B

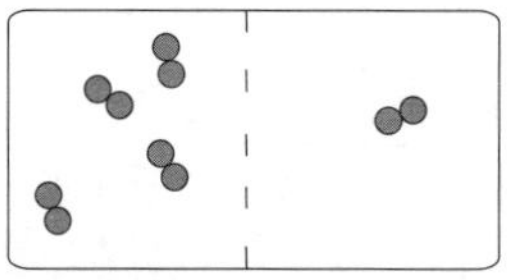

Would you expect the molecules to diffuse from left to right across the membrane **faster** in situation A or B? Explain your answer.

....

....

Q6 Phil was investigating the diffusion of **glucose** (a small molecule) and **starch** (a large molecule) through a **membrane**. He placed equal amounts of glucose solution and starch solution inside a bag designed to act like a cell membrane. He then put the bag into a beaker of water.

a) After an hour, Phil tested the water for the presence of starch and glucose. Circle which of the following you would expect to be found in the water outside the bag:

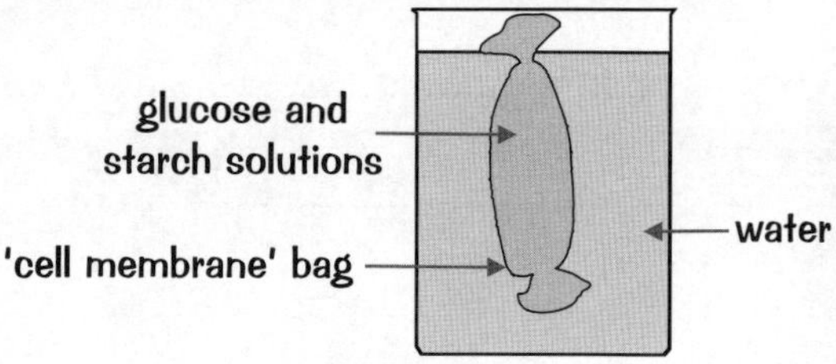

glucose **starch**

b) Explain your answer to part **a**).

....

....

c) Phil did the experiment again using the same amounts of glucose and starch solutions. This time he used a much longer, thinner bag.

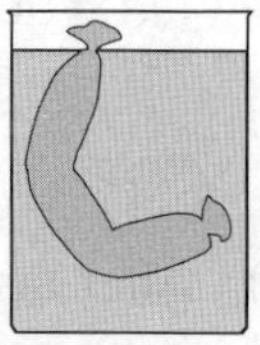

Will the diffusion happen faster or more slowly this time? Explain your answer.

....

....

Think about the surface areas of the bags.

Top Tips: Don't forget — diffusing molecules aren't all heading directly towards areas of lower concentration. They're all moving randomly, which makes them spread out evenly after a while.

Leaves and Diffusion

Q1 Name the parts labelled **A – E** to complete the diagram of a **leaf** below.

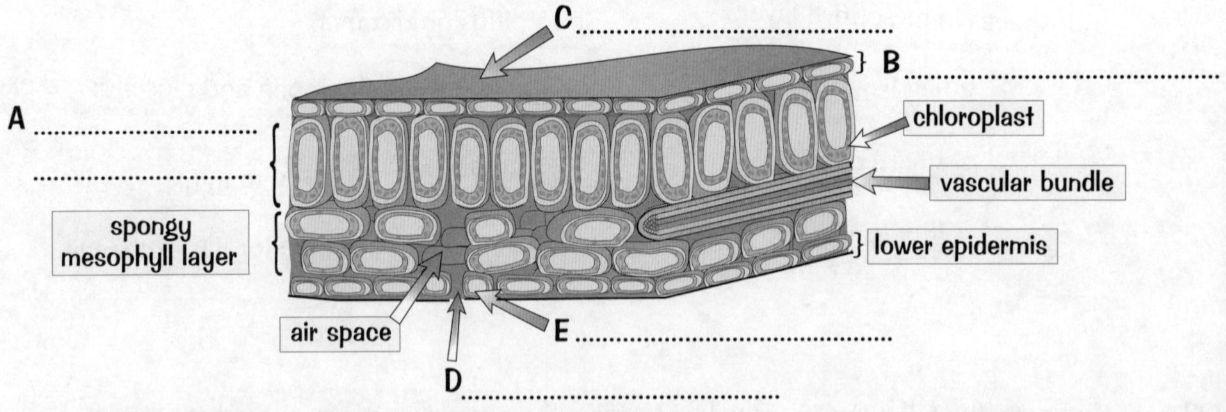

Q2 Answer the following questions about **gas exchange** in leaves.

a) Which process in the leaf uses CO_2 and produces O_2? ....

b) Which process in the leaf uses O_2 and produces CO_2? ....

Q3 Jill decides to do an experiment with her new fish tank before she puts the fish in.

She puts some **aquatic plants** in the tank and places it by the window. She then measures the concentration of **carbon dioxide** in the water over a period of 24 hours. She plots a graph of her results.

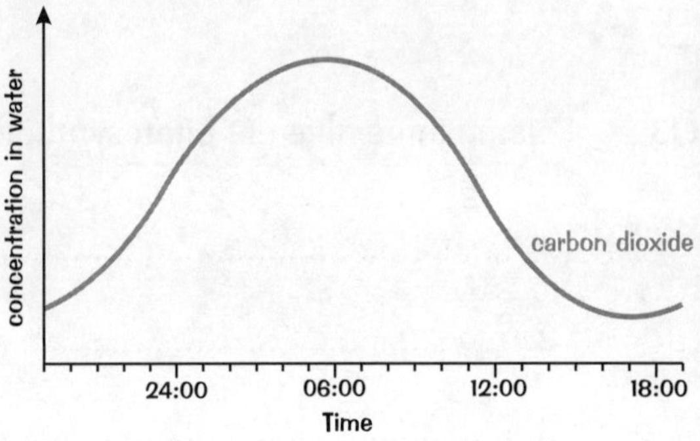

a) What **process** causes the carbon dioxide concentration to increase between 19:00, when Jill started the experiment, and 05:00?

....

b) Why do the plants need to carry out this process all the time?

....

c) Explain why the carbon dioxide concentration falls between 06:00 and 17:00.

....

d) Jill also measures the **oxygen** concentration in the water. Sketch another line on the graph to show how you would expect the oxygen concentration to change during Jill's experiment.

e) Explain your answer to part **d)**.

....

....

Leaves and Photosynthesis

Q1 Draw lines to match up the following **features** of a leaf with how they help with **photosynthesis**.

air spaces in mesophyll layer | short diffusion distance
broad leaves | control when stomata open and close for gas exchange
guard cells | large surface area exposed to light
thin leaves | large internal surface area for gas exchange

Q2 Complete the following passage by choosing the correct words from the list below.

transport	support	straw	vascular	blood	xylem

Leaves contain a network of .... bundles. These are the phloem and .... vessels. They .... water and glucose to and from the leaf, as well as helping to .... the leaf structure.

Q3 Name three different **photosynthetic pigments** found in plants.

1. ....

2. ....

3. ....

Q4 Explain how the following features make leaves well adapted to **absorb light** for photosynthesis.

a) different photosynthetic pigments

....

b) most chloroplasts arranged in the palisade layer

....

c) a transparent upper epidermis

....

Osmosis

Q1 Fill in the missing words to complete the paragraph.

diffusion **higher** **water** **lower** **membrane** **random** **partially**

Osmosis is the movement of .... molecules across a .... permeable .... from a region of .... water concentration (a dilute solution) to a region of .... water concentration (a concentrated solution). Osmosis is a special type of .... and is a consequence of the .... movement of individual water molecules.

Q2 Look at the diagram and answer the questions below.

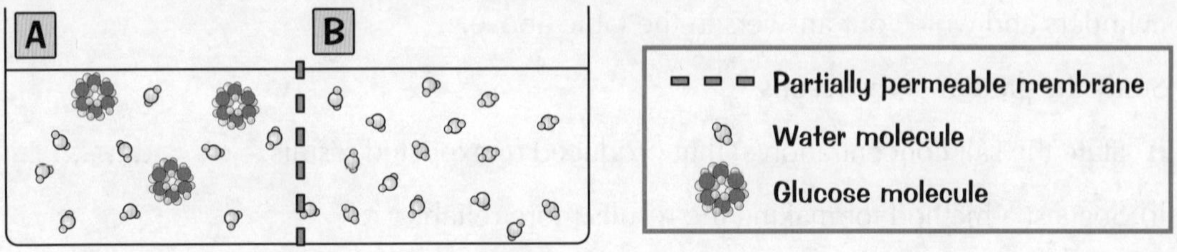

a) On which side of the membrane is there the highest concentration of water molecules? ....

b) What is a **partially permeable membrane**?

....

c) Predict whether the level of liquid on side B will **rise** or **fall**. Explain your answer.

....

....

Q3 A **red blood cell** is in some very **dilute** blood plasma.

a) Will water move into or out of the cell? Explain your answer.

....

....

Learning by osmosis

b) **i)** Describe what happens to an animal cell if it **takes in** too much water, and give the technical term for it.

....

ii) Describe what happens to an animal cell if it **loses** too much water, and give the technical term for it.

....

Osmosis

Q4 Some **potato cylinders** were placed in solutions of different **salt concentrations**. At the start of the experiment each cylinder was 50 mm long. Their final lengths are recorded in the table below.

Concentration of salt solution (molar)	Length of potato cylinder (mm)	Change in length of potato cylinder (mm)
0.0	60	
0.5	56	
1.0	50	
1.5	34	
2.0	45	

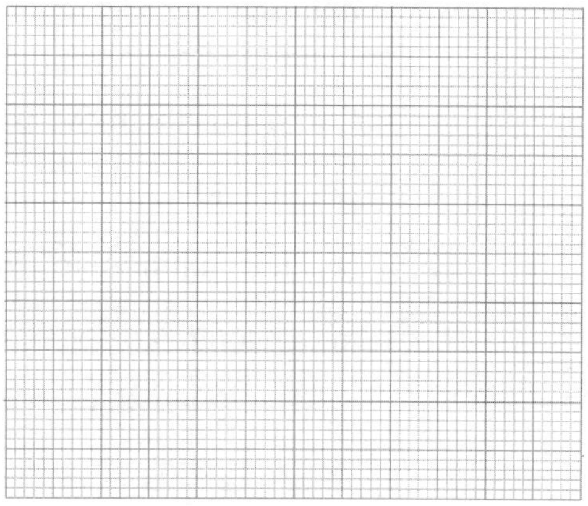

a) Plot a bar chart showing salt concentration and the final length of the potato cylinders.

b) Work out the change in length of each of the cylinders and write your answers in the table above.

c) Study the pattern of the results.

i) State the salt concentration(s) that produced unexpected results. ....

ii) Suggest a method for making the results more reliable.

....

d) Suggest **three** factors that should have remained constant to ensure that this was a fair test.

....

....

Q5 Plant cells look different depending on how much **water** they contain.

a) Use the words in the box below to describe the states of the following cells.

plasmolysed	**turgid**	**normal**	**flaccid**

A .... B .... C .... D ....

b) Explain why plants start to wilt if they don't have enough water.

....

....

c) Explain why the cell in diagram D hasn't totally lost its shape.

....

Transport Systems in Plants

Q1 Put the following statements under the **correct heading** in the table.

transport water

made of living cells

transport substances up the stem

transport substances both up and down the stem

transport food

made of dead cells

Xylem vessels	Phloem vessels

Q2 The diagram shows a cross-section of a **leaf**.

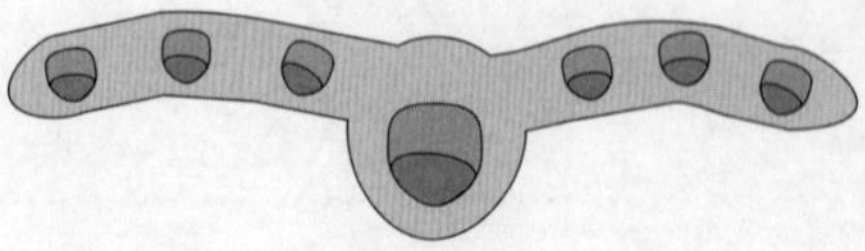

a) Label a **xylem vessel**, and a **phloem vessel** on the diagram.

b) Circle a **vascular bundle** on the diagram.

Q3 The diagram shows a cross-section of a **plant's stem**.

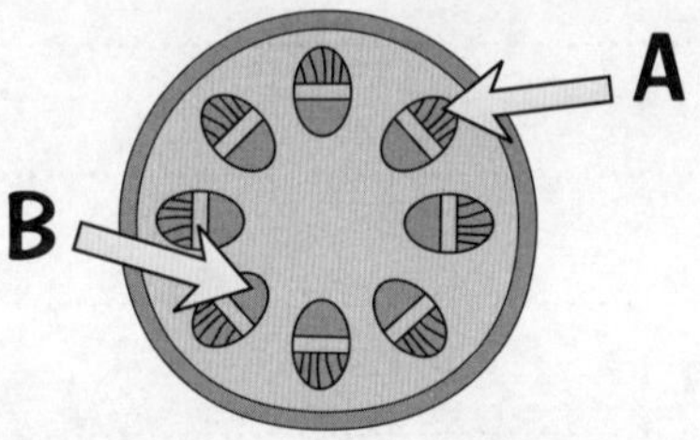

a) Name parts A and B.

A = ...

B = ...

b) Describe the function of **A** in the stem.

....

c) Describe one way that a cross-section of a root would look different from the cross-section of a stem.

....

Q4 Answer the following questions about **xylem**.

a) Name **two** substances transported by the xylem. ....

b) Describe the structure of a xylem tube.

....

....

Water Flow Through Plants

Q1 Complete this diagram of a **plant** according to the instructions given below.

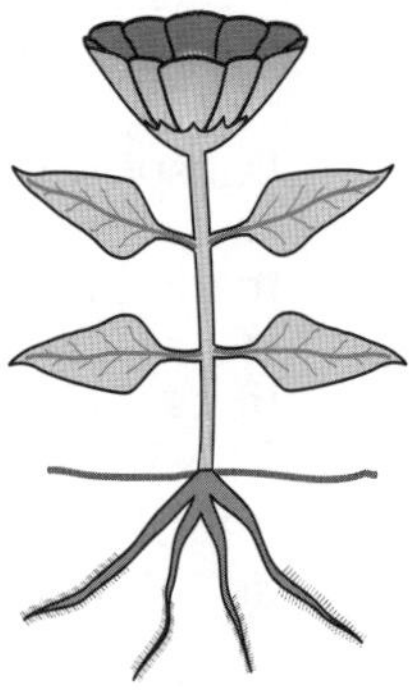

a) Put an **X** on the diagram to show one place where water enters the plant.

b) Add a **Y** to the diagram to show one place where water leaves the plant.

c) Add arrows to the diagram to show how water moves from where it enters to where it leaves.

Q2 **Root hair cells** are found on the roots of plants.

a) Draw a diagram of a root hair cell in the box provided.

b) Describe how water is drawn into this cell.

....

....

Q3 Give four ways that transpiration **benefits** plants.

1. ....
2. ....
3. ....
4. ....

Each word can only be used once.

Q4 Choose from the following words to complete the passage.

leaves evaporation roots flowers photosynthesis
phloem diffusion transpiration xylem stem

Most water leaves plants through the .... by the processes of .... and .... of water vapour. This creates a slight shortage of water in the ...., which draws water from the rest of the plant through the .... vessels. This causes more water to be drawn up from the .... This whole process is called .... It's a side effect of the way leaves are adapted for ....

Water Flow Through Plants

Q5 Indicate whether each of the following statements is **true** or **false**.

		True	False
a)	The transpiration rate decreases as the temperature increases.	☐	☐
b)	The more intense the light, the faster the transpiration rate.	☐	☐
c)	Transpiration happens more slowly when the air is humid.	☐	☐
d)	As the wind speed increases, the rate of transpiration decreases.	☐	☐

Q6 Explain the effect of increasing **temperature** on **transpiration rate**.

....

....

Q7 Plants need to **balance** water loss with water gain.

a) Give two ways that plants are adapted to reduce water loss from their leaves.

1. ....

2. ....

b) Suggest one way plants in hot climates adapted to reduce water loss.

Hint: Think about the stomata.

....

Q8 The diagram shows an **open stoma** and a **closed stoma**.

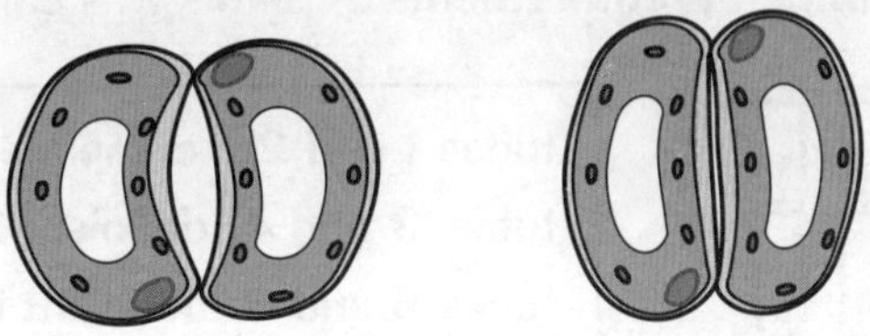

a) Label the following: **open stoma**, **flaccid guard cell**, **turgid guard cell**, **closed stoma**

b) Circle the correct word(s) in each pair to complete the sentences below.

i) When the guard cells are **turgid** / **flaccid** the stoma opens.

ii) The stoma closes when the guard cells are **turgid** / **flaccid**.

iii) Stomata **open** / **close** at night and when water supply is **high** / **low**.

c) Would you expect a plant's stomata to be open or closed on a bright sunny morning? Explain your answer.

....

....

Minerals Needed for Healthy Growth

Q1 Draw lines to match the following **minerals** with their **functions** in plants.

MAGNESIUM	for making amino acids and proteins
NITRATES	for making chlorophyll
PHOSPHATES	for making DNA and cell membranes
POTASSIUM	for helping enzymes to function

Q2 Spring has arrived but Pat has noticed that his **tomato crop** is **not** growing well and the plants have yellow older leaves.

a) Suggest a cause of both the poor plant growth and yellow older leaves.

....

b) Pat has been offered some **manure** for his field. The table shows the mineral content of different manures.

Which type of manure would you recommend Pat use? Explain your answer.

....

....

Material	% Nitrogen	% Phosphorus	% Potassium
Bullock manure	0.6	0.1	0.7
Cow manure	0.4	0.1	0.4
Horse manure	0.6	0.1	0.5
Pig manure	0.4	0.1	0.5
Poultry manure	1.0	0.4	0.6
Sheep manure	0.8	0.1	0.7

Q3 An investigation into the **mineral requirements** of plants was carried out as shown below.

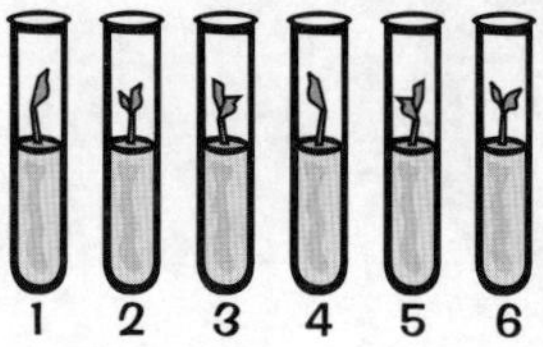

tubes 1 and 2: complete mineral supply
tubes 3 and 4: deficient in phosphates
tubes 5 and 6: deficient in magnesium

a) Suggest why tubes 1 and 2 were included.

....

b) Predict how the seedlings in the following tubes will grow:

i) 3 and 4 ....

ii) 5 and 6 ....

c) Suggest why a sufficient amount of all the minerals except one was supplied to tubes 3, 4, 5 and 6.

....

....

Minerals Needed for Healthy Growth

Q4 Natalie measures the **magnesium** level in the soil in her orchard every year. The graph below shows how the magnesium level in the soil changed over the ten year period from 2000 to 2010.

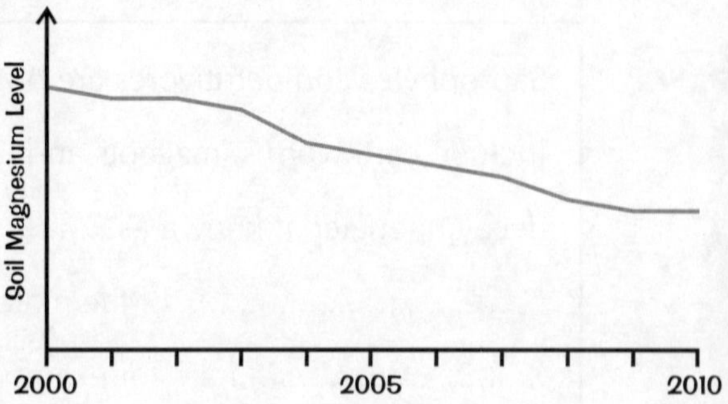

a) Describe the general trend shown in the magnesium level over the ten year period.

....

b) What do plants need magnesium for?

....

....

c) How could Natalie identify plants **deficient** in magnesium?

....

....

Q5 A diagram of a **specialised plant cell** is shown.

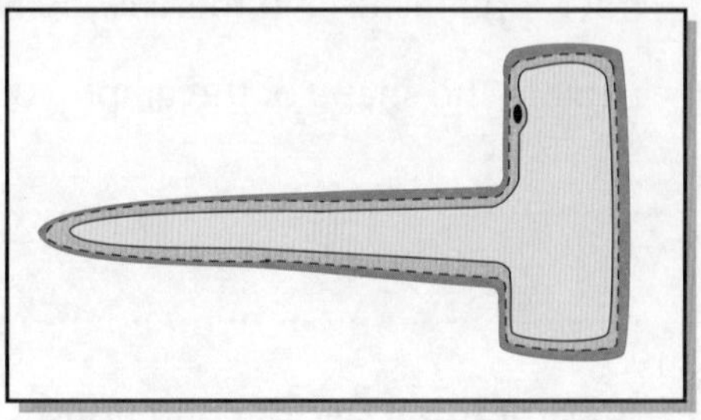

a) Name the type of cell shown.

....

b) What is the main **function** of this type of cell?

....

c) How is this type of cell adapted for its function?

....

d) Explain why minerals are **not** absorbed from the soil by **diffusion**.

....

e) Explain how these specialised cells absorb mineral ions from the soil. Use the words **active transport**, **concentration**, **respiration** and **energy** in your answer.

....

....

Top Tip: Whenever you're talking about molecules moving into or out of cells, you need to stop and think. They could be moving by **osmosis**, **diffusion** or **active transport** — it all depends on what type of molecule they are and whether they're moving up or down the concentration gradient.

Decay

Q1 Use the words provided to fill in the gaps in the paragraph below.

saprophytes **surface area** **extracellular** **detritivores** **woodlice** **detritus** **rabbits**

Saprophytes and detritivores are both types of decomposers. ....
include earthworms, maggots and .... They feed on dead and
decaying material known as .... As they do this, they increase the
.... of the material, which helps other decomposers to digest it.
...................................., for example fungi, also feed on dead material — but they
secrete digestive enzymes to break their food down by .... digestion.

Q2 Most decomposition is carried out by microorganisms. The **rate** of decay depends on three main things — **temperature**, **moisture** and **oxygen**.

a) Sketch a line on the graph provided to show what you think will happen to the rate of decay as **temperature increases**. (Assume the temperature doesn't rise enough to damage the microorganisms and there is plenty of water and oxygen.)

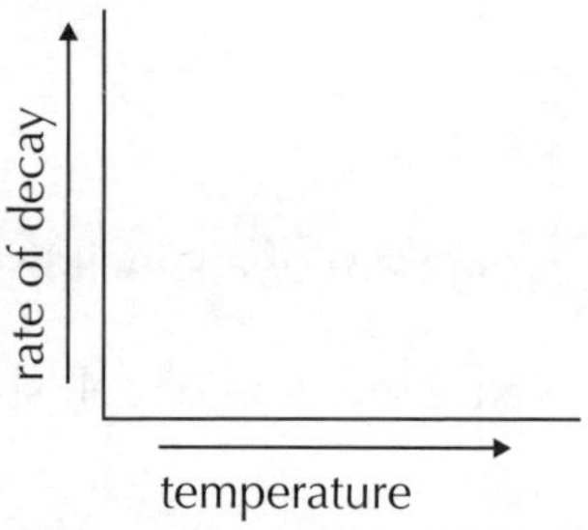

b) Explain the shape of the graph you have drawn.

....

....

c) A list of **three** sets of conditions is shown in the box. **Rank** the sets of conditions from 1 to 3, 1 being the best for decay and 3 being the worst for decay.

Conditions	Rank
Dry, cold, no oxygen	....
Moist, warm, oxygen	....
Moist, cold, no oxygen	....

Q3 Draw lines to link the **food preservation methods** with how they reduce decay.

Canning	the acidic conditions kill any decomposers
Freezing	decomposers need water, so can't survive
Pickling	decomposers can't reproduce at such low temperatures
Drying	keeps decomposers out

Q4 Explain how storing tuna in **brine** (salt water) helps to preserve it.

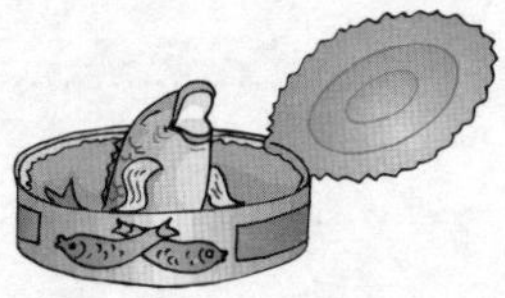

....

Top Tip: It's easy to remember the methods we use to **stop** decomposers — as long as you know about the conditions microbes like for decay. So make darn well sure you've learnt them...

Intensive Farming

Q1 Match up each **intensive farming** method below with the correct description and advantage.

using herbicides	kills insects	less energy wasted on movement and keeping warm
using insecticides	animals kept in small pens	more energy from the Sun is used by the crops
battery farming	kills weeds	less energy is transferred to another food chain

Farmer Giles' methods were intense

Q2 **Plants** can be grown without soil.

a) What is the name of this technique?

....

b) What are the plants grown in?

....

c) Give an example of a plant that is often grown in this way.

....

d) Some of the things that need to be considered for this technique are listed below.
Tick to show whether each is an **advantage** or **disadvantage**.

Feature	Advantage	Disadvantage
i) No soil to anchor roots and support the plants.	☐	☐
ii) Lots of fertilisers need to be added.	☐	☐
iii) Diseases can be controlled more effectively.	☐	☐
iv) Mineral levels can be controlled more accurately.	☐	☐

Q3 Many people feel that **battery farming** animals is **unethical**.

a) Give one argument against battery farming.

....

b) Describe one other **ethical dilemma** that is raised by an aspect of intensive farming.

....

....

Pesticides and Biological Control

Q1 **Pesticides** are chemicals that are used to kill pests.

Write down two problems that can be caused by the use of pesticides.

1. ....

2. ....

Q2 **Cockroaches** were sprayed with a **pesticide** to control the size of their population.

Explain what effect this could have on the rest of the food web shown.

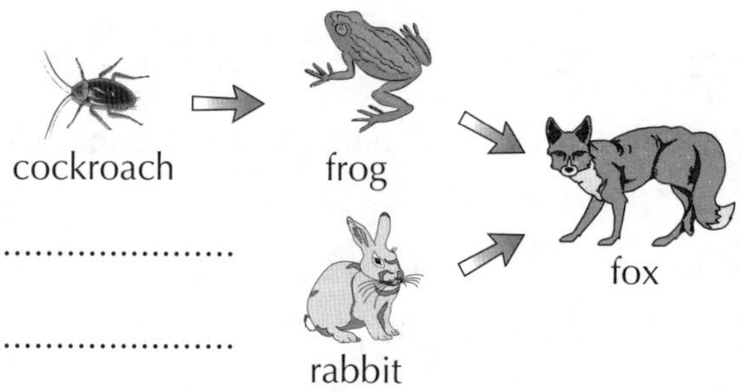

....

....

....

Q3 **Biological control** is an alternative to using pesticides.

a) What is biological control?

....

b) Write down two **advantages** and two **disadvantages** of using biological control.

Advantage 1: ....

Advantage 2: ....

Disadvantage 1: ....

Disadvantage 2: ....

Q4 **Pesticides** that were being sprayed onto fields near to a bird of prey's habitat were found in the birds in **toxic** levels.

Birds of prey only eat other animals.

a) Suggest how pesticide that was sprayed onto crops was found in the birds.

....

b) The amount of pesticide sprayed onto the field was carefully controlled to ensure it was at the lowest concentration that would kill the pests. Suggest why the birds contained such large amounts of the pesticide.

....

....

Alternatives to Intensive Farming

Q1 For each of the **intensive farming methods** below suggest an **organic farming alternative** and give one **advantage** of the alternative method.

a) **Using insecticides:** alternative method — ....

Advantage: ....

b) **Using herbicides:** alternative method — ....

Advantage: ....

c) **Using chemical fertilisers:** alternative method — ....

Advantage: ....

Q2 Describe the following organic farming methods and explain how they work.

a) Varying seed planting times

....

....

b) Crop rotation

....

....

....

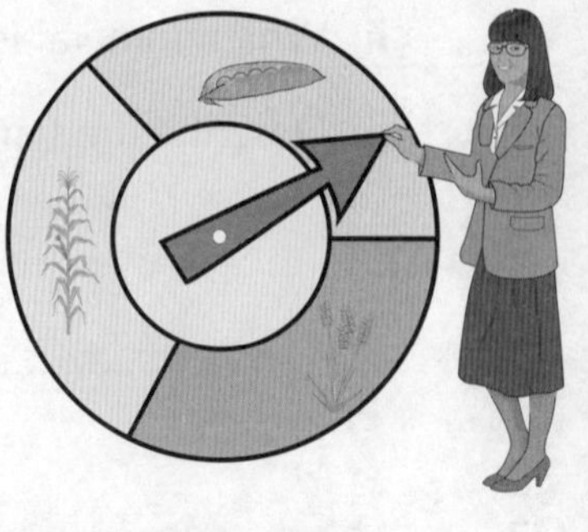

Q3 Complete the following passage about **organic farming**, using the words from the list below.

wildlife	drawbacks	expensive	space	less	workers

Although organic farming methods have their obvious advantages, they also have several .... Organic farming methods take up more .... than their intensive alternatives, meaning that less land can be set aside for .... and other uses. Organic farming requires more .... (who all need to be paid), so organic produce is more .... in the shops. Organic farming methods also produce much .... food than can be produced using intensive farming techniques.

Mixed Questions — Module B4

Q1 Farmer MacDonald uses **chemical pesticides** on his crops.

a) Explain why he uses these chemicals.

....

b) What effect might the use of these pesticides have on the **buzzards** in the following food chain?

Apple tree → caterpillars → blackbirds → buzzards

....

....

c) Some chemical pesticides are **persistent**. What does this mean?

....

d) Farmer MacDonald also puts **fertiliser** on his crops. The fertiliser he uses provides the crops with essential minerals to ensure healthy growth.

i) Which **two** minerals are most important for photosynthesis?

....

ii) Which mineral is vital for making proteins? ....

iii) Describe the symptoms of a plant with **potassium deficiency**.

....

....

Q2 The diagram below shows a cross section through a plant root.

a) Draw arrows to link up each label to the correct part of the root.

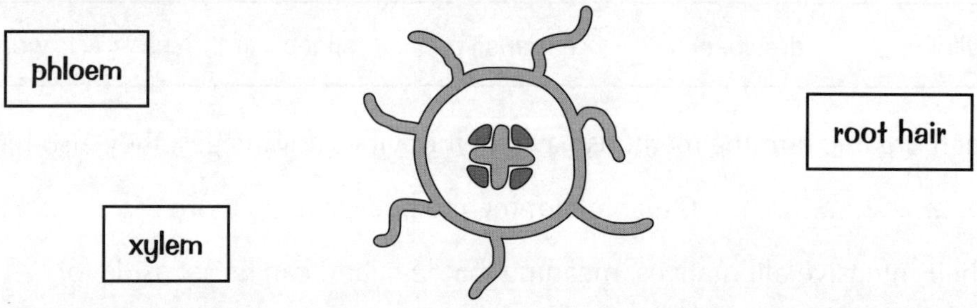

b) Complete the sentences below by circling the correct word(s) from each pair.

The concentration of minerals in the soil is **lower / higher** than in root hair cells. As a result, minerals can't be absorbed by **diffusion / active transport** — instead they're absorbed by **diffusion / active transport**. This requires energy from **photosynthesis / respiration** because the minerals have to be moved against the concentration gradient.

Mixed Questions — Module B4

Q3 A student carried out a series of experiments on **osmosis**.

a) Give a definition of the word 'osmosis'.

....

....

b) In the first experiment potato chips were placed in different solutions. Their mass was recorded at the start and again after one day. The results are shown in the following table.

tube	start mass, g	end mass, g
A	1.20	1.45
B	1.40	1.21
C	1.32	1.32

Which tube (A, B or C) contained:

i) pure water? ....

ii) dilute sugar solution? ....

iii) concentrated sugar solution? ....

c) **i)** In the second experiment **water** loss from a leafy shoot was measured. The shoot was exposed to **different conditions** and the water loss measured each time. The results are shown on the graph. Complete the table to show which line represents each set of conditions.

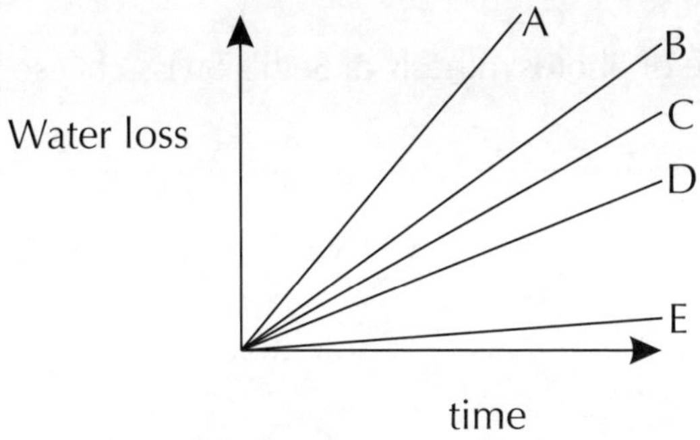

Treatment	Line
kept in normal conditions	C
covered, clear plastic bag	
fanned, cool air	
fanned, warm air	
covered, black plastic bag	

ii) Explain the effect of **humidity** on transpiration rate.

....

....

....

Mixed Questions — Module B4

Q4 **Legumes** are plants that have nodules on their roots containing **nitrogen-fixing bacteria**.

a) Suggest why some farmers include legumes in their crop rotations.

....

b) Explain how and why an insufficient nitrogen intake affects a plant's development.

....

....

Q5 Seth investigated the effect of different concentrations of **carbon dioxide** on the rate of photosynthesis of his Swiss cheese plant. The results are shown on the graph below.

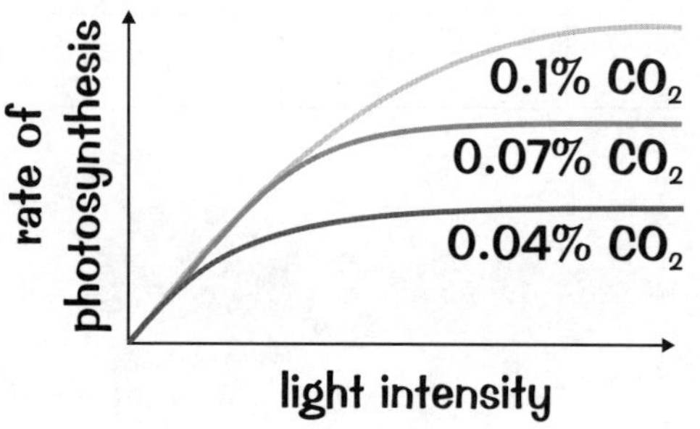

a) Describe how increasing the concentration of CO_2 affects the rate of photosynthesis.

....

....

b) Name one other factor that would affect the rate of photosynthesis of Seth's Swiss cheese plant.

....

c) Explain why the graph levels off eventually.

....

....

d) Give three features of leaves that make them well adapted to the **diffusion** of carbon dioxide.

1. ....

2. ....

3. ....

Bones and Cartilage

Q1 Vertebrates have an **internal skeleton** whereas insects have an external one. Give three advantages of an internal skeleton.

1. ....

2. ....

3. ....

Q2 The diagram below shows a **long bone**.

a) Name the parts **A**, **B** and **C** on the diagram.

A .... B .... C ....

b) What is part **A** covered with?

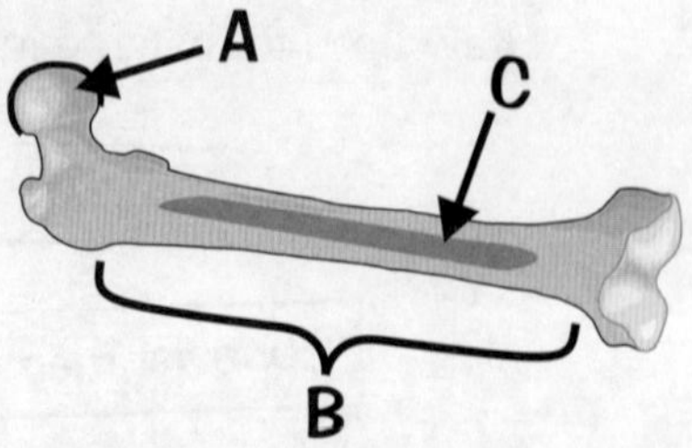

....

c) Long bones are **hollow**. Give one **advantage** of this.

....

....

Q3 Complete the passage about **bones** and **cartilage** using the words below.

infected	cartilage	knock	grow	calcium	phosphorus	broken	bone	repair	ossification

Bones and cartilage are made up of living cells — this allows them to .... and .... themselves, but it also means that they can become ....

Bones are strong, but they can be .... by a sharp ....

In the womb, bones start off as cartilage. They turn to bone when .... and .... are deposited as you grow. This process is called ....

In people who are still growing, there is a lot of .... present.

Q4 Elderly people often suffer from a disease called **osteoporosis**. Their bones are more prone to **fractures**.

a) Why are their bones more likely to break?

....

....

b) Explain why you should try to avoid moving anyone who might have a fracture.

....

Joints and Muscles

Q1 Complete the passage below to explain how different **joints** allow different ranges of movement.

socket	hinge	ball	rotate	one

.... joints, such as the knee and elbow, allow movement in .... direction only. .... and .... joints, for example the hip and shoulder, allow movement in many directions — they can also ....

Q2 Draw lines to match each part of a **synovial joint** to its function.

Cartilage	Hold the bones together
Synovial membrane	Acts as a shock absorber
Ligaments	Lubricates the joint
Synovial fluid	Produces synovial fluid

Q3 The diagram on the right is of a human **arm**.

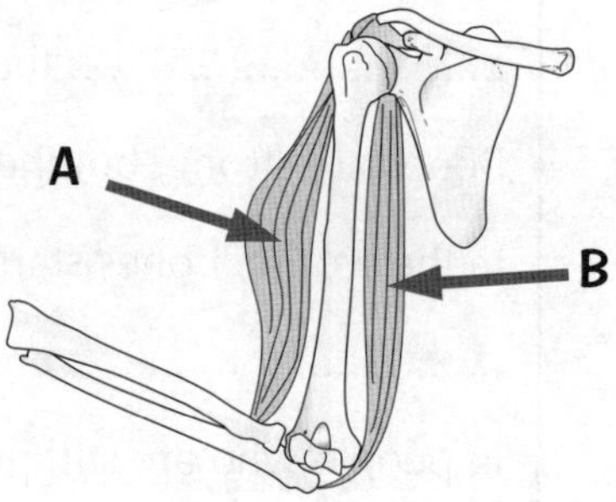

a) Name the muscles **A** and **B** on the diagram.

A .... B ....

b) Name the part of the arm that acts as a **pivot**.

....

c) Give the letter of the muscle that is **contracted** in the diagram. ....

d) Give the letter of the muscle that is **relaxed** in the diagram. ....

e) Describe how the antagonistic muscles A and B cause the arm to **straighten**.

....

Top Tips: There are loads of different types of joints but you only need to know about two — hinge, and ball and socket... so get them learnt. Don't forget that muscles usually work in pairs.

Circulatory Systems

Q1 Complete the passage using the words provided below.

diffusion small oxygen large circulatory glucose slow waste fast

The cells of all living organisms need to be supplied with .... and .... They also need to get rid of .... like carbon dioxide. Single-celled organisms are small enough that these materials can move in and out by ...., but multicellular organisms are so .... that diffusion would be too .... Because of this, they need a .... system to move materials more efficiently around the body.

Q2 Complete the sentences below by circling the correct word(s) from the choices given.

a) Arteries carry blood **away from** / **towards** the heart under **low** / **high** pressure.

b) Veins carry blood **away from** / **towards** the heart under **low** / **high** pressure.

Q3 The diagram below shows how **blood pressure** changes as blood flows around the body.

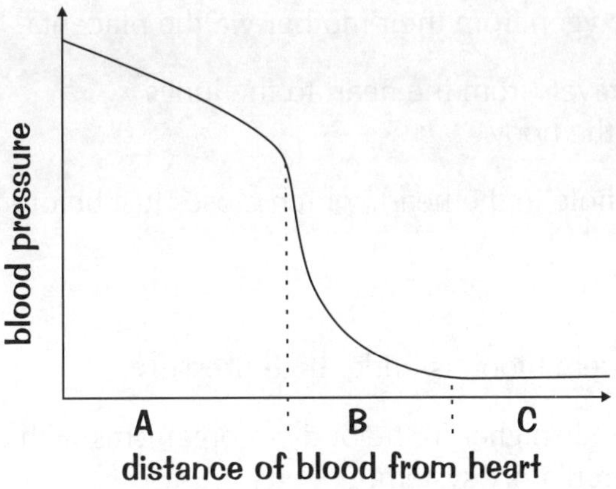

Blood was under a lot of pressure revising for his exams.

a) What happens to blood pressure as blood flows away from the heart?

....

b) Name the types of blood vessels **A**, **B** and **C** on the diagram.

A .... B .... C ....

Circulatory Systems

Q4 Organisms can have a **single** or **double** circulatory system.

a) Draw lines to match each organism to the correct type of circulatory system and its description.

fish	single circulatory system	two circuits of blood vessels from the heart
mammals	double circulatory system	one circuit of blood vessels from the heart

b) **i)** Explain why organisms with a **single circulatory system** have a **two-chambered heart**.

....

....

ii) Explain why organisms with a **double circulatory system** have a **four-chambered heart**.

....

....

Q5 Tick the boxes next to the following statements to show whether they're **true** or **false**.

		True	False
a)	Unborn babies don't need a double circulatory system.	☐	☐
b)	Unborn babies get their oxygen from their mother via the placenta.	☐	☐
c)	In unborn babies, blood travels from the heart to the lungs and then on to the rest of the body.	☐	☐
d)	All unborn babies have a hole in the heart, which closes just before birth.	☐	☐

Q6 In a double circulatory system blood is under **high pressure**.

a) Explain why blood pressure is higher in the body of organisms with a double circulatory system than those with a single circulatory system.

....

....

....

b) Give one **advantage** of having higher blood pressure.

....

The Cardiac Cycle and Circulation

Q1 The **cardiac cycle** is the sequence of events that takes place in one complete heartbeat.

The sentences below describe some of these events. Number them to show their correct order.

The first one has been done for you.

- [ ] Blood flows into the pulmonary artery and aorta.
- [1] Blood flows into the atria from the vena cava and pulmonary vein.
- [ ] The ventricles contract.
- [ ] The cycle starts again as blood flows into the atria.
- [ ] The atria contract, pushing blood into the ventricles.

Q2 For each of the following stages of the cardiac cycle, tick the boxes to show whether the semilunar and atrio-ventricular valves are **open** or **closed**.

a) Blood flows into the atria.

	Open	Closed
Semilunar valves		
Atrio-ventricular valves		

b) The ventricles contract.

	Open	Closed
Semilunar valves		
Atrio-ventricular valves		

c) The atria contract.

	Open	Closed
Semilunar valves		
Atrio-ventricular valves		

Q3 We understand how the circulatory system works thanks to the work of **William Harvey**.

a) Give **two** things that William Harvey discovered.

....

....

b) How did Claudius Galen's idea of how the circulatory system works differ from Harvey's idea?

....

....

....

....

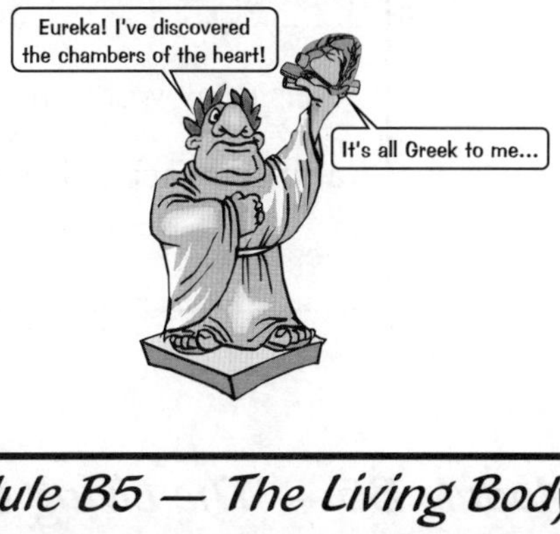

Heart Rate

Q1 Your **heart rate** changes depending on your level of activity.
The graph below shows the heart rate of a student who sprints for a bus.

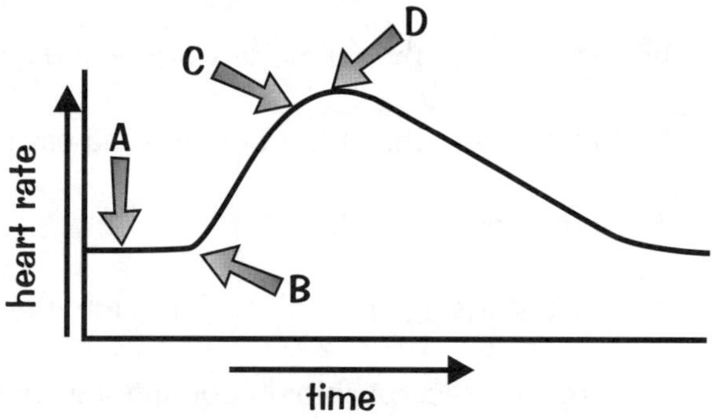

After a brisk walk in the countryside, Kate's art rate increased dramatically.

a) i) At what point, **A**, **B**, **C** or **D**, does he start to run?

....

ii) At what point, **A**, **B**, **C** or **D**, does he stop running?

....

b) Suggest an **advantage** of an increased heart rate during sprinting.

....

c) Which **hormone** can also cause your heart rate to increase?

....

Q2 Complete the passage about the **heart's pacemaker**, using the words below.

Some words may be used more than once.

skin	SAN	muscle	electric current	atria	AVN	wire	contract	ventricles

A small .... is generated by the .... The current spreads through the .... cells of the .... making them .... The current then stimulates the .... to produce an .... This current spreads through the .... cells of the .... making them .... In this way, the .... always contract before the .... If the pacemaker cells don't work properly the .... can be generated by an artificial pacemaker implanted under the .... and connected to the heart by a ....

Heart Rate

Q3 The diagrams below show **ECG recordings** from a healthy person and a person admitted to hospital with a heart problem.

a) What is recorded by the ECG trace?

....

b) Which parts of the cardiac cycle do the labels **A**, **B**, **C** and **D** represent?

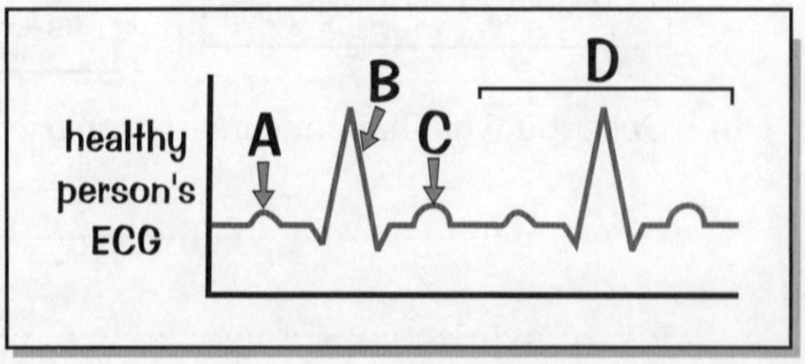

A ....

B ....

C ....

D ....

c) How does the ECG trace of the hospital patient **differ** from that of the healthy person?

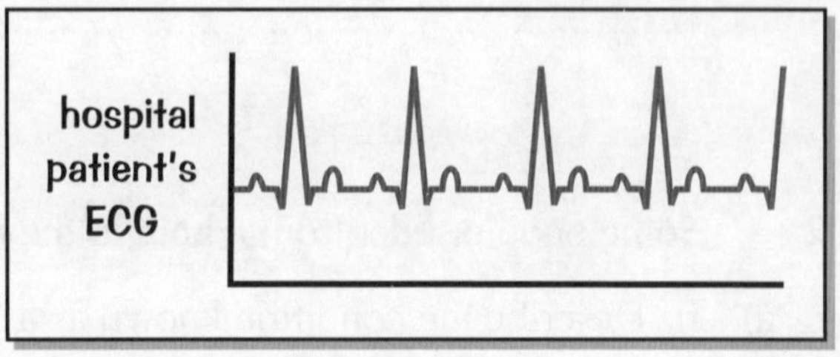

....

....

d) Give one heart problem an ECG is commonly used to detect.

....

Q4 **Echocardiograms** can also be used to investigate heart function.

a) What is an echocardiogram? Tick the correct box.

- [ ] An X-ray of the heart.
- [ ] A way of measuring the blood pressure of the heart chambers.
- [ ] An ultrasound scan of the heart.

b) Suggest one heart problem that echocardiograms can be used to detect.

....

Top Tips: There could well be a question on ECGs in the exam so it's crucial that you know what they are used for, how to label one and how to identify different problems from them.

Heart Disease

Q1 **Surgery** is often used to correct heart problems.

a) Draw lines to match each heart condition to the problems it causes and the correct treatment.

Valve damage	reduces blood flow to the heart muscle	coronary bypass surgery
Coronary Heart Disease	blood doesn't circulate as effectively as normal	replacement by artificial valves

b) Describe what happens in a **coronary bypass** operation.

....

....

c) When might a **heart assist device** be used?

....

Q2 Some people suffer from a **hole in the heart**.

a) **i)** Describe the condition known as a 'hole in the heart'.

....

ii) What effect can it have on the circulation of blood in the heart?

....

b) Explain how a hole in the heart results in less oxygen in the blood.

....

c) How can a hole in the heart be corrected?

....

Q3 **Heart pacemakers** and **valves** can be used to treat heart disease instead of a heart transplant.

a) Give **one advantage** of fitting heart pacemakers and valves compared with heart transplants.

....

b) Give **one disadvantage** of fitting heart pacemakers and valves compared with heart transplants.

....

Blood Clotting and Transfusions

Q1 When you are cut, your blood **clots** so that you don't lose too much.

a) What is a **blood clot**?

....

b) How is a blood clot **formed**?

....

....

Q2 Use the words below to complete the passage about **blood clotting disorders**.

heparin **haemophilia** **inherited** **warfarin** **prevent** **aspirin**

Strokes and DVT are conditions caused by excessive blood clotting. People at risk of these conditions take drugs such as .... , ... and .... to help .... blood clotting.

.... is an .... disease in which the blood takes longer to clot. It can be treated with injections of a clotting factor.

Q3 There are four different **blood groups**, which are determined by the **antigens** present on a person's red blood cells.

a) Name the **four** blood groups. ....

b) What is an **antigen**?

....

c) What is **agglutination**?

....

d) Where in the blood are **antibodies** found?
Tick the correct answer.

- [ ] On red blood cells
- [ ] On the platelets
- [ ] In the plasma

Blood Clotting and Transfusions

Q4 Complete the table below to show which blood groups have which **antigens** and which **antibodies**.

Blood group	Antigens present	Antibodies present
		anti-B
	B	
AB		
	none	

Q5 The presence or absence of blood group antigens determines who can receive **blood transfusions** from certain donors.

a) In what situation might you need a blood transfusion?

....

b) Circle the correct answer to show whether a person can **receive** or **donate** a particular blood group.

Use the table you have just filled in to help you.

i)	If they are blood group **A** can they **receive** blood group **B**?	**yes / no**
ii)	If they are blood group **A** can they **receive** blood group **O**?	**yes / no**
iii)	If they are blood group **AB** can they **receive** blood group **B**?	**yes / no**
iv)	If they are blood group **AB** can they **donate** to blood group **B**?	**yes / no**

c) Which blood group can donate their blood to any other blood group? ....

d) Which blood group can only receive blood of the same blood type? ....

e) Explain why a person with blood group A can't accept blood from a person with blood group B.

....

....

Q6 When blood is donated it is collected in a bag containing a substance called **heparin**.

Suggest a reason why heparin is present.

....

Top Tips: You might be asked to interpret data on blood transfusions in the exam — don't panic, think about the antigens and antibodies present and draw a table if it helps you figure it out.

Transplants and Organ Donation

Q1 Both living and dead people can donate organs but have to meet certain **criteria** to do so.

a) **i)** Name an organ that could be donated by a living donor. ....

ii) Give **two** criteria that living donors must meet to donate an organ.

....

b) Describe the criteria that a dead person must meet to donate an organ.

....

....

Q2 Complete the passage by choosing from the words below.

skill	drugs	age	success	rejection	organ	surgery

Transplants are risky in general because they involve major .... but .... rates depend on a lot of factors. The type of .... transplanted is important, as are the .... of the patient and the .... of the surgeon. Even if all goes well there can be problems caused by .... or by taking immuno-suppressive ....

Q3 The table below shows the number of **heart transplants** carried out in Cloudyford.

Year	1996	1997	1998	1999	2000	2001	2002	2003	2004	2005
No. heart transplants	36	35	35	31	30	27	24	21	26	20

a) Plot these figures as a bar chart on the grid on the right.

b) Describe how the number of heart transplants has changed over time.

....

....

c) Suggest why the future number of transplants carried out in Cloudyford may:

i) increase. ....

ii) decrease. ....

Organ Donation and Organ Replacement

Q1 There **aren't enough donors** to provide organs for all the people who need them.

a) Tick the boxes next to the factors below that explain why there are problems in the supply of organs.

☐ There's a shortage of people willing to be donors.

☐ Some donated organs will be the wrong colour.

☐ Not all donated organs will be the right tissue match for the patient who needs them.

☐ Patients are picky about which organs they'll accept.

☐ Donors must be roughly the same size and age as the patient who needs their organs.

b) Some countries have a **register** of people willing to donate organs after their death.

i) Suggest one **advantage** of having a register of donors.

....

ii) Suggest one **problem** with a register of donors.

....

Q2 Temporary **mechanical replacement organs** can be used to keep people alive.

a) Give **one** example of a temporary mechanical replacement for an organ.

....

b) Give four **problems** with using mechanical replacements for organs.

1. ....

2. ....

3. ....

4. ....

Top Tips: The average waiting time for an adult kidney transplant in the UK is around three years. Waiting times for different organs vary, but all are affected by the shortage of organ donors.

The Respiratory System

Q1 Complete the following sentences by circling the correct word in each pair.

a) Carbon dioxide is **beneficial** / **toxic** to the body at a **low** / **high** level.

b) When the **brain** / **nose** detects a rise in the carbon dioxide level it responds by **decreasing** / **increasing** the rate of breathing.

Q2 The following statements describe events which take place during either **inspiration** (breathing in) or **expiration** (breathing out):

- Intercostal muscles and diaphragm contract
- Thorax volume increases
- Air is pushed out of the lungs
- Pressure in lungs increases
- Pressure in lungs decreases
- Thorax volume decreases
- Diaphragm and intercostal muscles relax
- Air enters the lungs

Place the statements into the correct columns in the right order.

Inspiration	Expiration

Q3 Doctors measure **lung capacity** to help diagnose and monitor lung diseases.

a) What **machine** do they use to measure lung capacity? ....

b) What is the total volume of air you breathe in during a normal breath called? ....

c) What is **vital capacity air**? ....

d) At point **A** on the graph draw:

i) One normal breath in.

ii) Then one big breath out.

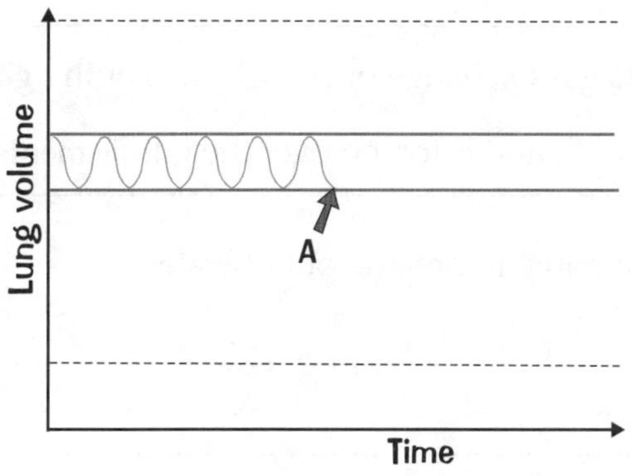

More on the Respiratory System

Q1 Gas exchange in humans occurs in the **alveoli**.

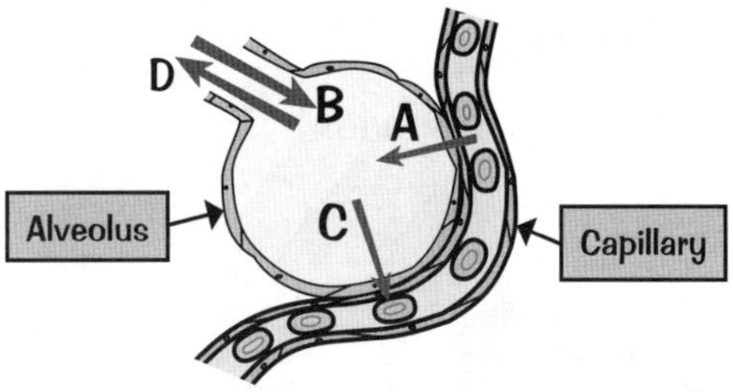

a) Match the labels A-D with the following statements:

i) air in ☐

ii) air out ☐

iii) movement of CO_2 ☐

iv) movement of O_2 ☐

b) By what **process** does the exchange of oxygen and carbon dioxide occur?

....

Q2 The alveoli are adapted to ensure **efficient** gas exchange.

Describe **four** features of the alveoli which make gas exchange as efficient as possible.

1. ....

2. ....

3. ....

4. ....

Q3 **Amphibians** and **fish** have different methods of gas exchange from humans.

a) **i)** How do adult **amphibians** exchange oxygen and carbon dioxide?

....

ii) How and why does this restrict where they can live?

....

....

b) **i)** Complete the paragraph by circling the correct words.

In **fish** / **reptiles** gas exchange occurs at the **mouth** / **gills**. Water rich in oxygen flows in through the mouth and is forced over the gill **filaments** / **fibres** when the mouth closes.

ii) Why are **fish** unable to breathe out of water?

....

....

Lung Disease

Q1 The respiratory tract is lined with a **mucous membrane**.

a) What is the function of the following?

i) Mucus ....

ii) Cilia ....

b) Name two parts of the respiratory tract where the mucus and cilia are found.

1. .... 2. ....

c) The respiratory tract leads to the lungs. Why are the lungs particularly prone to infection?

....

Q2 Lung diseases have many causes. For the following diseases give a **cause** (e.g. lifestyle, industrial or genetic) and describe the illness.

a) Cystic fibrosis ....

....

b) Asbestosis ....

....

c) Lung cancer ....

....

Q3 Complete the following passage about **asthma** by filling in the blanks using the words below.

wheezing	lining	difficult	inhaler	inflamed	contract	a tight chest	muscles

Asthma sufferers' lungs are overly sensitive to things such as pollen or dust. These cause the .... of the airways to become .... and fluid to build up in the airways. The .... around the bronchioles ...., narrowing the airways and making it .... to breathe. Symptoms include shortness of breath, ... and .... To control attacks asthmatics take drugs , usually administered by an ....

Digestion

Q1 Tick the box next to the statement which is **true**.

- [ ] Small soluble molecules in food need to be assembled into large molecules before they can pass into your blood plasma or lymph.
- [ ] Large insoluble molecules in food need to be broken down into small molecules, so they can pass more easily into your blood plasma or lymph.
- [ ] Large insoluble molecules in food need to be broken down into small molecules, so they can pass more easily into your intestines.

Q2 Complete the table to show where the following **digestive enzymes** are active in the body.

	Active in...	Also active in...
Carbohydrases		
Proteases		
Lipases		

Q3 Fill in the boxes to show how the **three main food groups** are **broken down** during digestion.

a)

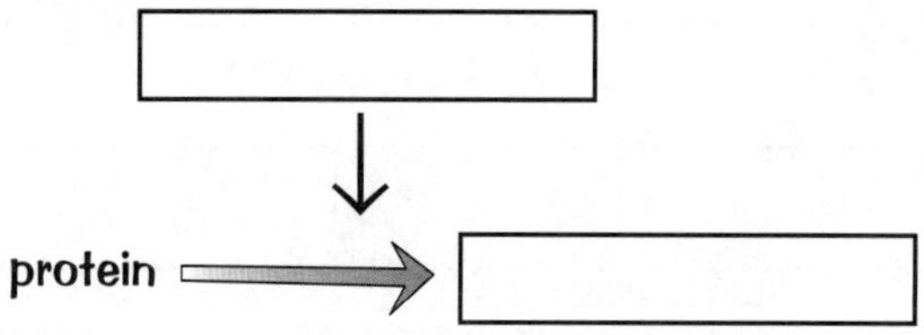

Start digesting sooner with Lipase Lipstick.

b)

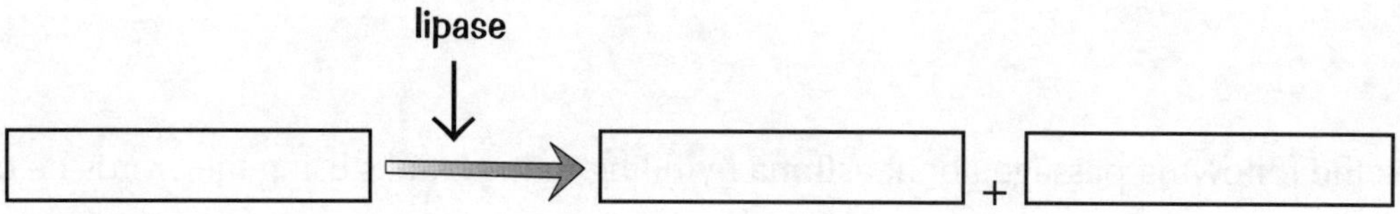

c)

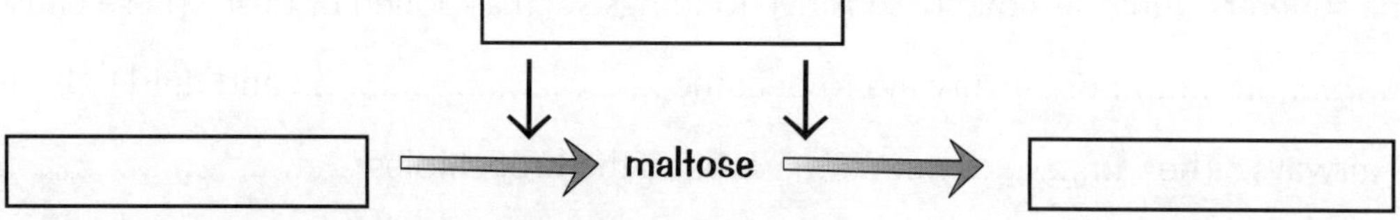

Q4 Explain the importance of **physical digestion**.

....

....

More on Digestion

Q1 Use the words provided to complete the passage below.

alkaline	protease	small intestine	acidic

The pH in the stomach is very .... It's maintained at this level to provide the optimum pH for .... enzymes. Other enzymes have different optimum pHs and so need different conditions — for example, the mouth and .... are .... so the enzymes found there can function properly.

Q2 Circle the correct word(s) in each pair to complete this passage about **bile**.

Bile is stored in the **gall bladder** / **pancreas** before being released into the small intestine.

Bile **acidifies** / **neutralises** the material from the stomach so that it is the optimum pH for the **enzymes** / **microorganisms** in the rest of the digestive system to work.

Bile also helps digest **fat** / **glycerol** by breaking it down into tiny droplets.

This is called **emulsification** / **reduction** and it gives a much bigger surface area for **carbohydrase** / **lipase** enzymes to work on.

Q3 Describe how the products of **digestion** move into the blood and lymph.

....

....

....

Q4 Describe two features of the **small intestine** that make it well-adapted to the absorption of food.

1. ....

....

2. ....

....

Top Tips Digestion is about getting all the **nutrients** from your food into your blood. The nutrients need to be broken down into **small molecules** first, so that they can be easily absorbed.

The Kidneys

Q1 The diagram below shows the human **kidneys**. The renal vein has been labelled. Complete the remaining labels **a)** to **d)**.

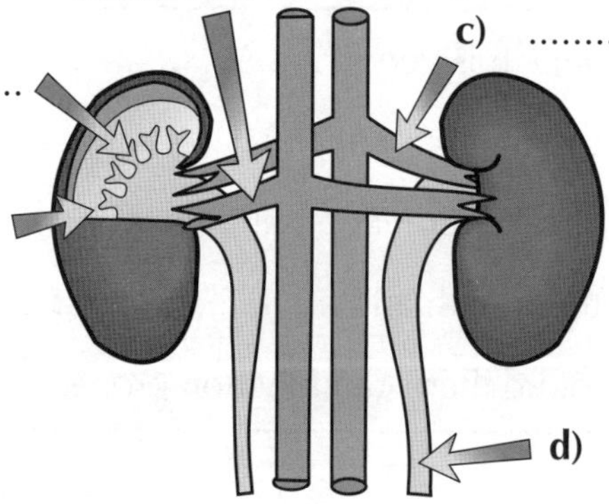

Q2 The kidney is involved in the **excretion** of wastes from the body. One of these wastes is **urea**.

a) **i)** Where is urea produced?

....

ii) What is urea produced from?

....

b) Briefly explain how the kidneys excrete wastes from the body.

....

c) What is the end product of excretion?

....

Q3 Complete the passage using some of the words provided below.

glomerulus selectively proteins salt
randomly urea nephron ADH capsule

Some words may be used more than once.

Water, ... and salt are squeezed out of the blood and into the .... under high pressure. Membranes between the blood vessels in the .... and the .... act like filters, so big molecules like proteins are not squeezed out. As the liquid flows along the .... useful substances are .... reabsorbed.
How much water is reabsorbed is regulated by the hormone ....
.... is also .... reabsorbed.

Waste Removal

Q1 The concentration of water in the blood is adjusted by the **kidneys**. They ensure that the water content never gets **too high** or **too low**.

a) What is the name given to the **mechanism** by which water content is regulated?

....

b) Complete the diagram below by circling the correct word in each pair.

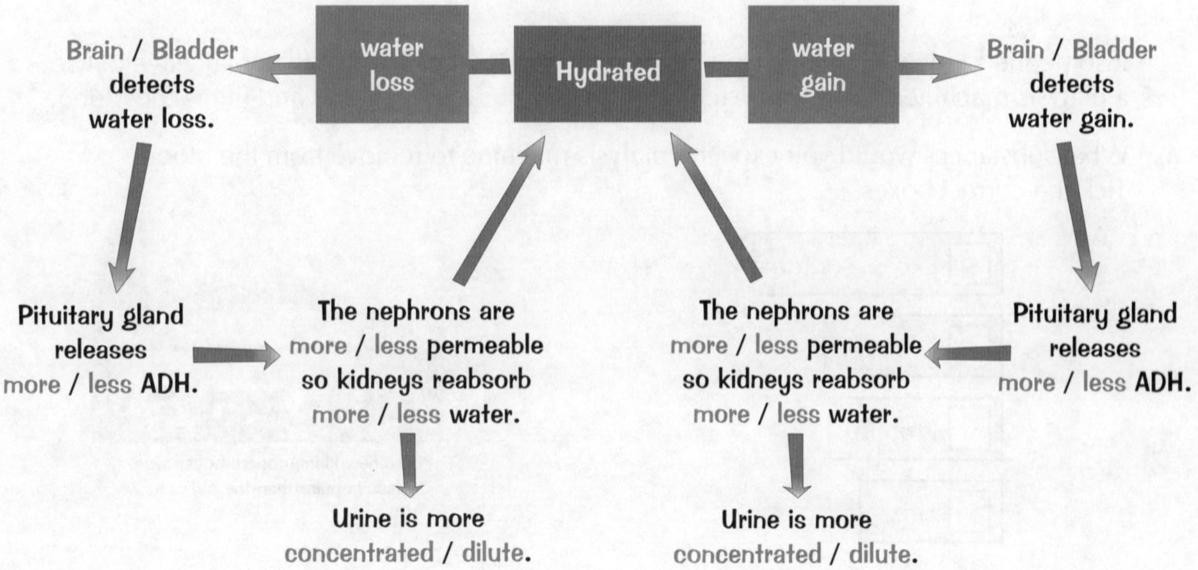

Q2 The concentration of urine and amount of urine produced are affected by many factors.

a) List three things that determine the **amount** and **concentration** of urine.

1. ....

2. ....

3. ....

b) Complete the following sentences by circling the correct words.

i) When you drink too little you will produce **more concentrated** / **less concentrated** urine.

ii) On a hot day you will produce **more concentrated** / **less concentrated** urine than on a cold day.

iii) Drinking a lot of water will produce a **large** / **small** amount of urine.

iv) Drinking a lot of water will produce **dilute** / **concentrated** urine.

v) Exercising will produce **more concentrated** / **less concentrated** urine than resting will.

c) Why does **exercising** change the concentration of urine produced?

....

....

Waste Removal

Q3 Explain why it's important to keep the concentration of water molecules in the blood plasma **constant**.

....

....

Q4 If someone's kidneys fail they may be given a **kidney transplant** or they may have to use a **dialysis machine**. A dialysis machine does the job of the kidneys and filters the blood.

a) What substances would you expect a dialysis machine to remove from the blood? Tick the correct boxes.

- ☐ Excess sodium
- ☐ Glucose
- ☐ Proteins
- ☐ Urea

The new kidney opera house was less popular than the old one.

b) Add the correct labels to the dialysis diagram.

A Blood returned to patient

B Dialysis fluid in

C Selectively permeable barrier

D Dialysis fluid out

E Blood from patient

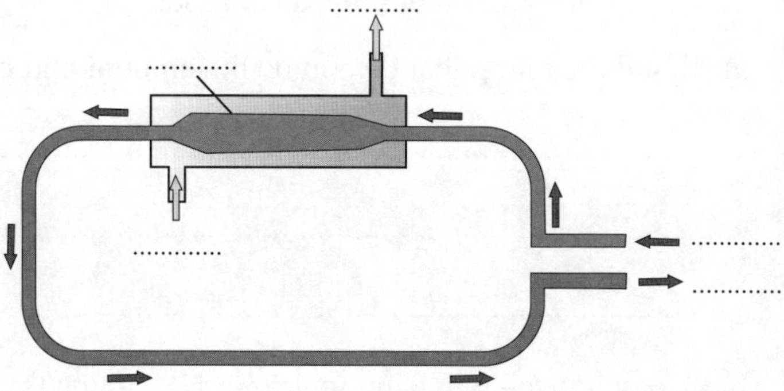

c) **i)** **How** does the composition of dialysis fluid compare with the composition of blood plasma?

....

ii) Why is this important?

....

Top Tips: Dialysis is a clever technique that's saved lives. The problem is that it can take up to four hours to filter the blood and it has to be done a couple of times a week. An alternative is a kidney transplant — you can live with only one kidney, so it's possible for some people with kidney failure to receive a donated organ from a member of their family.

The Menstrual Cycle

Q1 The menstrual cycle is controlled by four hormones: **FSH**, **LH**, **progesterone** and **oestrogen**.

a) Complete the table below to show the effects of these by placing ticks in the correct boxes.

Effect	FSH	LH	Progesterone	Oestrogen
Causes the lining of the uterus to repair (thicken and grow)				
Causes egg to develop in ovaries				
Controls ovulation				
Maintains uterus lining				

b) Which of the hormones above are released by the pituitary gland?

....

c) What do the following letters stand for?

i) FSH: ....

ii) LH: ....

Q2 When the concentration of one hormone becomes too high, the release of another hormone returns it to a lower level.

a) What is the name given to the **mechanism** by which hormones involved in the menstrual cycle are controlled?

....

b) Draw lines to complete the following sentences.

Progesterone inhibits the release of	progesterone.
Oestrogen inhibits the release of	oestrogen.
LH indirectly stimulates the production of	LH.
FSH stimulates the ovaries to produce	FSH.

Controlling Fertility

Q1 A variety of infertility treatments are available to help people who can't conceive naturally.

a) Tick the correct boxes to show whether the following statements about infertility treatments are **true** or **false**.

	True	False
i) Artificial insemination can use sperm from a donor.	☐	☐
ii) For artificial insemination to be successful the couple must still have sex.	☐	☐
iii) If a woman has low levels of FSH she would be given an ovary transplant.	☐	☐
iv) Women with no ovaries can receive an ovary transplant.	☐	☐
v) Women who can't produce eggs can have a baby using donated eggs.	☐	☐

b) Write out correct versions of the false statements below.

....

....

Q2 The **pill** is an **oral contraceptive** that contains oestrogen. Explain how it is used to reduce fertility.

....

....

....

Q3 Doctors can screen a foetus for **genetic diseases** before it's born by looking at its **DNA**.

a) Complete the following passage using the words provided.

needle	Down's Syndrome	fluid	amniocentesis	chromosomes

In ...., a long .... is used to remove some of the .... surrounding the foetus. This contains skin cells from the foetus and the .... in these can be analysed. This method can be used to identify conditions like ....

b) Explain why foetal screening raises ethical issues.

....

....

....

Controlling Fertility

Q4 Some couples who can't conceive naturally use **in vitro fertilisation (IVF)** to have a child.

a) Tick the box next to the correct description of IVF.

- A man's sperm is placed into a woman's uterus. ☐
- A healthy ovary is transplanted into a woman. ☐
- A woman's eggs are fertilised outside of the body. ☐
- A woman is injected with fertility hormones. ☐

b) Suggest one thing that needs to be healthy for IVF to be successful.

....

c) During a course of IVF treatment, **why** would a woman be given FSH injections?

....

d) What is meant by the term **surrogate mother** and when would one be used?

....

....

....

e) State the main risk associated with IVF.

....

f) Not all of the eggs that are fertilised are implanted into the woman's uterus.

i) What happens to the ones that are not implanted?

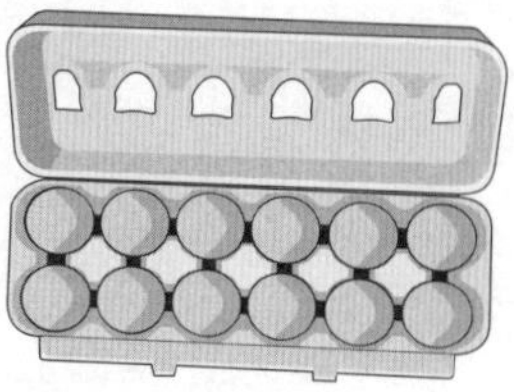

....

....

ii) Why do some people disagree with this?

....

g) Give **one** argument in favour of infertility treatments such as IVF.

....

More on Growth

Q1 Growth is stimulated by a hormone known as **growth hormone**.

a) Where in the body is growth hormone produced? Circle the correct answer.

pancreas   liver   adrenal gland   pituitary gland   reproductive organs

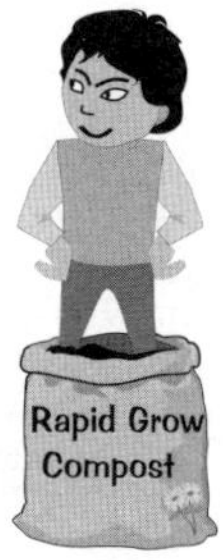

b) Fill in the missing words to complete the sentence below:

Human growth hormone stimulates general ....,
especially in the ....

Q2 Give two things that can cause extremes in human height.

1. ....

2. ....

Q3 Describe how **exercise** can influence growth.

....

....

Q4 A baby's growth was recorded. The results are shown on the **growth chart** below.

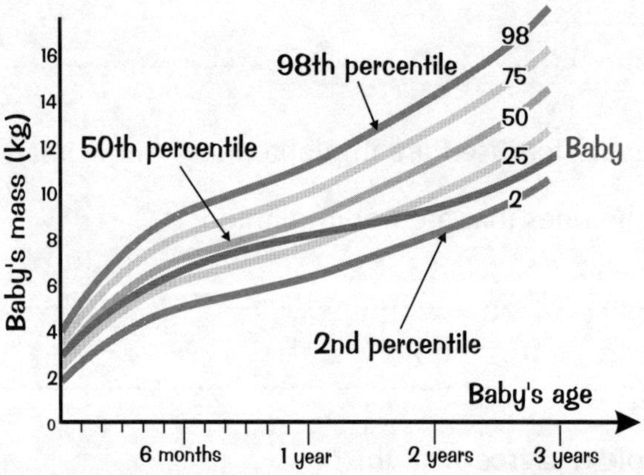

Would a doctor be concerned about the growth of this baby? Explain how you decided.

....

....

....

More on Growth

Q5 Over the past 100 years or so **life expectancy** in the UK has **increased** dramatically.

a) The boxes below contain changes that have occurred over this period and the result they have had. Match up the pairs by drawing a line between them.

People are financially better off

Previously fatal conditions can now be treated

Medical advances

Safer and healthier environment

Improved working and housing conditions

Healthier diet and lifestyle

b) State **two** problems associated with an increase in population.

....

....

Q6 Tick the boxes next to the statements to show whether they are **true** or **false**.

	True	False
a) All the parts of a foetus and baby grow at the same rate.	☐	☐
b) All the parts of a foetus grow at the same rate, but different parts of babies grow at different rates.	☐	☐
c) Different parts of a foetus and baby grow at different rates.	☐	☐

Q7 Zapphites have a similar growth pattern to humans. The graph shows the **head circumference** (size) of baby Zapphites between birth and 40 weeks. The shaded area shows where 90% of babies fall.

Baby's name	Age (weeks)	Head circumference (cm)
Charles	19	46.5
Edward	15	51
Engletree	34	54
George	27	49
Henry	23	49
Oliver	29	57
Richard	39	50
Xionbert	23	51.5

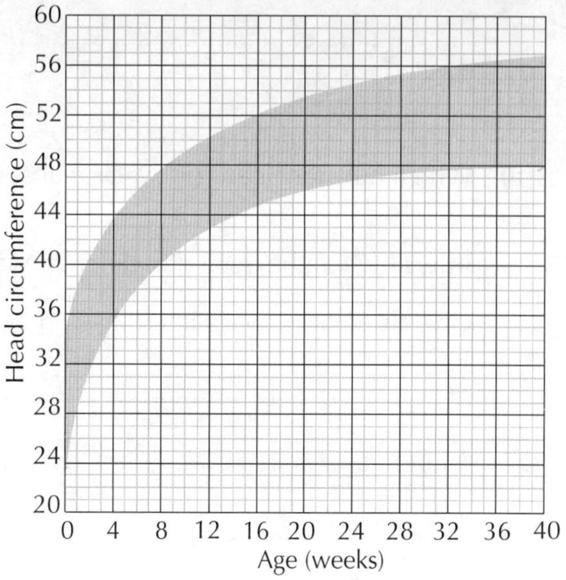

a) Plot the head circumferences of the above babies.

b) Which baby's head size may cause concern? ....

Zapphites come from the planet Zaphron.

c) Why might Zapphite doctors monitor a baby's head circumference?

....

Mixed Questions for Module B5

Q1 James was in a car crash and had a suspected **hip fracture**.

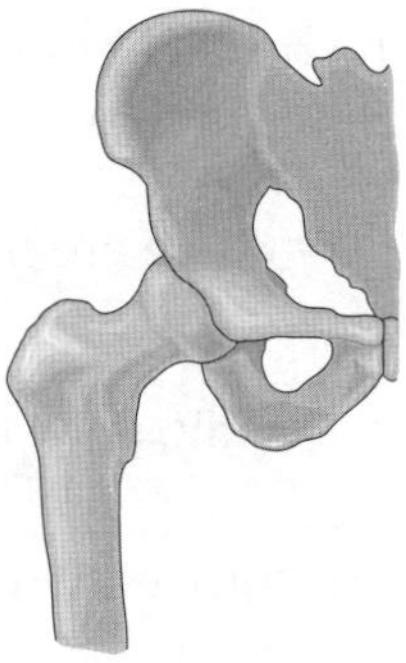

a) What **type** of joint is the hip joint?

....

b) What is the range of movement in this type of joint?

....

....

c) What holds the bones together at the joint?

....

d) James was taken to **surgery** to have the fracture pinned. He needs a **blood transfusion** whilst in surgery. He is blood group B. Which blood groups can he receive?

....

Q2 Your **heart rate** changes when you **exercise**.

a) Describe how your heart rate varies when you exercise.

....

b) Which **cells** control how fast the heart beats? ....

c) Exercise also affects how much **urine** you produce. Explain **why** it affects urine production.

....

....

d) Which **hormone** controls water reabsorption in the kidneys? ....

Q3 **Infertility** can be treated in different ways. A recently developed way is an **ovary transplant**.

a) Give **three** other ways infertility can be treated.

1. ....

2. ....

3. ....

b) To have an ovary transplant you need a **donated ovary**. The UK has a shortage of organ donors. Suggest how the organ donation system could be changed to increase the number of donors.

....

....

Mixed Questions for Module B5

Q4 The **kidneys** are responsible for **filtration** of the blood and **excretion** of waste from the body.

a) What are the three main roles that the kidneys perform?

1. ....

2. ....

3. ....

b) The table below shows the amounts of salt, sweat and urine lost by a particular person on a cold day, a hot day and a normal day. The same food and drink was consumed on each day and the same amount of exercise was done.

	salt in urine, g/day	salt in sweat, g/day	volume of urine, dm^3/day	volume of sweat, dm^3/day
cold day	**3.1**	**2.0**	**2.8**	**0.2**
hot day	**4.6**	**3.1**	**2.0**	**2.3**
normal day	**3.5**	**2.5**	**2.1**	**1.1**

i) In total, how much salt was lost on the cold day?

....

ii) Why is a greater volume of urine produced on a cold day than on a hot day?

....

....

c) If a person has kidney failure they are unable to filter their blood properly.
One solution is a kidney transplant. Give **two** problems with organ transplants.

....

....

d) In addition to organs, blood can also be donated.
Complete the table below to show which blood donors can give to which recipients.

Blood Group	Can give blood to	Can get blood from
A		
B		
AB		
O		

Think about the antigens on the surface of red blood cells

Mixed Questions for Module B5

Q5 A person's **lifestyle** choices can seriously affect their health.

a) Eating a lot of saturated fat can increase your risk of developing a **blocked coronary artery**. What happens when a coronary artery gets blocked?

....

b) Give two ways in which a doctor might investigate **heart function**.

1. .... 2. ....

c) Give an example of how **smoking** can affect the lungs.

....

d) Smoking can also decrease **lung capacity**. Lung capacity is measured using a **spirometer** which produces a **spirogram**.

On the diagram, which letter corresponds to:

i) tidal air ....

ii) vital capacity ....

iii) one breath ....

iv) residual air ....

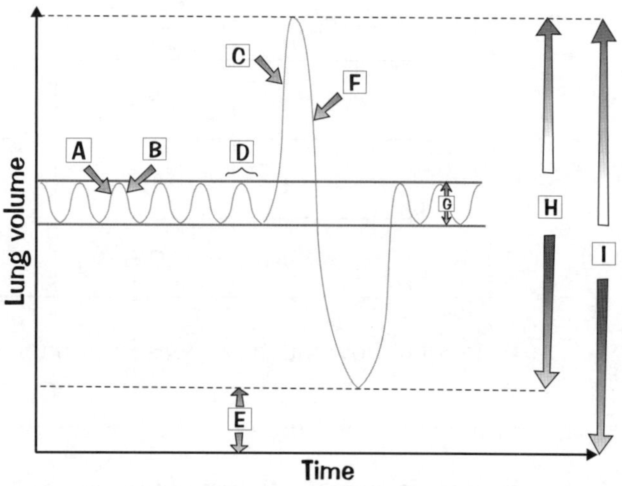

e) If a person's heart or lungs are damaged they can be replaced by donated organs. Describe two **ethical concerns** of organ donation.

1. ....

2. ....

Q6 The diagram represents the **menstrual cycle** in a particular woman.

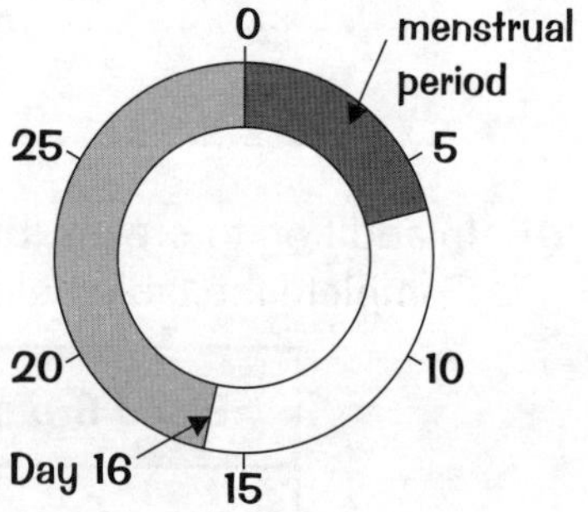

a) Oestrogen is one of the four main hormones that control the menstrual cycle. Give **two** functions of oestrogen.

....

....

b) Another key hormone in the menstrual cycle is FSH. Why is it unlikely that a woman with low levels of FSH will be able to get pregnant?

....

....

Mixed Questions — Module B5

Q7 The diagram shows the steps that occur from the entry of blood into the **kidneys** to the exit of blood from the kidneys. Write the letters A to E in the diagram to show the correct order.

A Wastes such as urea are carried out of the nephron, into the ureter and down to the bladder as urine.

B Small molecules are squeezed into the capsule. Membranes between the glomerulus and capsule act like filters so large molecules remain in the blood.

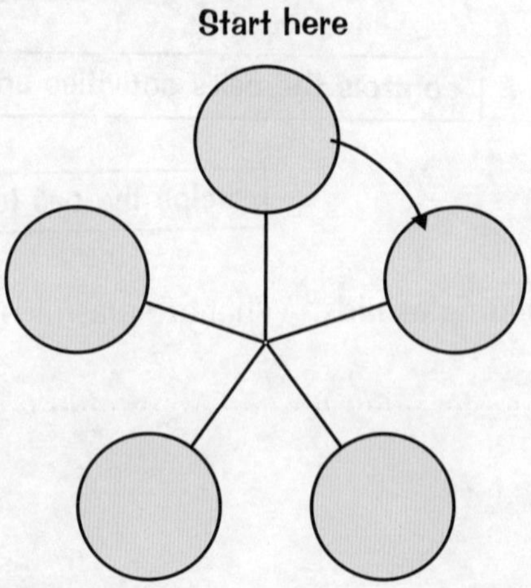

C Useful products are reabsorbed from the nephron and enter the capillaries.

D Molecules travel from the capsule along the nephron.

E Blood enters the kidney.

Q8 Charlotte fell off a swing and broke and cut her wrist. After about six weeks her wrist was fully healed.

a) Why are bones able to grow and heal themselves?

....

b) Describe how bone is formed from cartilage.

....

....

c) When Charlotte was a baby, her growth was recorded to make sure she was growing normally. What three measurements would have been taken?

1. ....

2. ....

3. ....

d) Describe how diet can influence a child's growth.

....

....

Bacteria

Q1 a) Draw lines to match up each **part** of a **bacterial cell** to its correct description.

DNA	maintains the cell's shape and helps to stop the cell from bursting
Flagellum	controls the cell's activities and replication
Cell wall	helps the cell to move

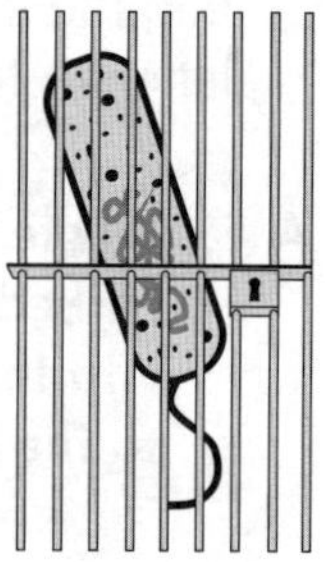

b) Some bacterial cells contain **plasmids**. What are plasmids?

....

Q2 Complete the passage below by choosing the correct word from each pair.

> Bacteria are found in four main shapes — rods, curved rods, **spheres / cones** and spirals. They reproduce by a process called binary **fission / fusion**. This is a type of **asexual / sexual** reproduction, which basically means that each bacterial cell splits in **two / three**. In **cool / warm** conditions, with plenty of nutrients available, bacteria can reproduce very quickly.

Q3 Bacteria can survive in a huge range of **habitats**.

a) Suggest three different habitats that bacteria can survive in.

....

b) Explain why bacteria are able to live in such a wide range of habitats.

....

....

....

Top Tips: You can't really expect to pick up too many marks in this module if you don't know the basics, so make sure you're happy with these first few pages before you get stuck in to the rest. And trust me, these bacteria aren't all as scary as you might think. Some even make yoghurt...

Bacteria

Q4 Complete the passage about **yoghurt making** by filling in the gaps using the words below.

packaged **flavours** **pasteurised** **lactic acid** ***Lactobacillus*** **sterilised** **incubated**

First, all the equipment is .... to reduce the risk of contamination. Then, to make the yoghurt, milk is .... to kill off any unwanted microorganisms. A starter culture of .... bacteria is added and the mixture is .... The bacteria break down the lactose sugar into .... This causes the milk to clot and form yoghurt. .... (such as fruit) and colours can then be added and the yoghurt is ....

Q5 In suitable conditions, bacteria can reproduce very quickly.

a) Explain how storing food in a **fridge** can help to stop it **going off** so quickly.

....

....

b) Explain why many **illnesses** are caused by bacteria that reproduce very quickly.

....

....

Q6 Raymond is culturing bacteria from his kitchen sponge on an **agar plate**.

a) Explain why Raymond should use **aseptic technique** when he's culturing the bacteria.

....

....

b) Describe the **aseptic techniques** that Raymond should use as he works.

....

....

....

Microorganisms and Disease

Q1 a) Complete the diagram of a **virus** by filling in the missing labels.

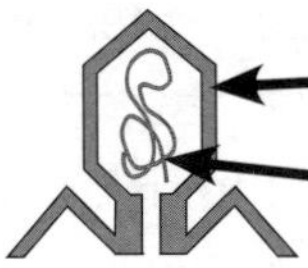

i) ....

ii) ....

b) In the spaces provided, write whether the following statements are **true** or **false**.

i) Viruses can only reproduce inside other living cells. ....

ii) A particular type of virus will only attack specific cells. ....

iii) Viruses only attack animal cells. ....

c) The diagram below shows how viruses reproduce. Add descriptions to each stage of the process.

i) .... ii) .... iii) ....

....

Q2 For each of the three **diseases** below, draw lines to indicate how they are **spread** and give one **method of prevention** for each disease.

DISEASE	HOW IT'S SPREAD	METHOD OF PREVENTION
Influenza	Food	....
Cholera	Water	....
Food poisoning	Airborne droplets	....

Q3 Developing countries often have a **higher incidence of cholera** than developed countries. Explain fully why you think this might be.

....

....

....

Treating Infectious Diseases

Q1 **Antiseptics** and **antibiotics** are used to help control disease.

a) What type of microbes are **unaffected** by antibiotics? ....

b) Give **one** feature that antiseptics and antibiotics have in common.

....

c) Give **two** differences between antiseptics and antibiotics.

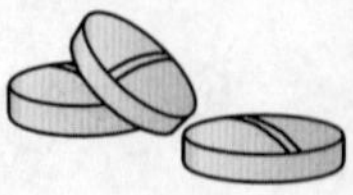

....

....

Q2 Explain what happens to **cause disease symptoms** once a microbe has entered the body.

....

....

....

Q3 There is concern about some bacteria developing resistance to antibiotics.

a) Put the stages in order (1-4) to show how a population of bacteria can develop **resistance** to a particular antibiotic through **natural selection**.

☐ The gene becomes more common in the population over time — giving the population resistance to the antibiotic.

☐ Bacteria with these mutated genes are more likely to survive and reproduce in a host being treated with the antibiotic.

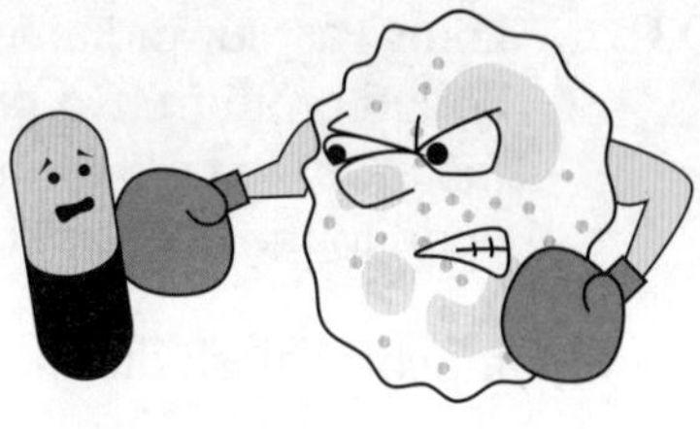

☐ Random mutations in bacterial DNA can lead to it being less affected by a particular antibiotic.

☐ The gene for antibiotic resistance will be passed on to lots of offspring.

b) **i)** Explain why doctors should **only prescribe** antibiotics when they're really **necessary**.

....

....

ii) State why it's always important to **complete a course** of antibiotics.

....

....

More on Infectious Diseases

Q1 Disease spreads rapidly after **natural disasters**.

Explain how each of the following can lead to ill health:

a) damaged sewage systems ....

....

b) damaged electrical supplies ....

....

c) displaced people ....

....

Q2 **Joseph Lister** and **Alexander Fleming** both made important contributions to **disease treatment**.

Decide whether the following statements about their work are **true** or **false**.

	True	False
a) Joseph Lister discovered the antibiotic penicillin in 1928.	☐	☐
b) Lister realised that infections of wounds were caused by microbes from the air.	☐	☐
c) A mould called *Penicillium notatum* produced the first antibiotic to be discovered.	☐	☐
d) The first antiseptic to be used was camomile acid.	☐	☐
e) Penicillin was discovered by accident when bacteria contaminated a plate of mould.	☐	☐

Q3 **Louis Pasteur** did an experiment in which he boiled broth in **two different flasks** and allowed the broth to cool. Both **Flask 1** and **Flask 2** were open to the air, but **Flask 2** had a **long curved neck**.

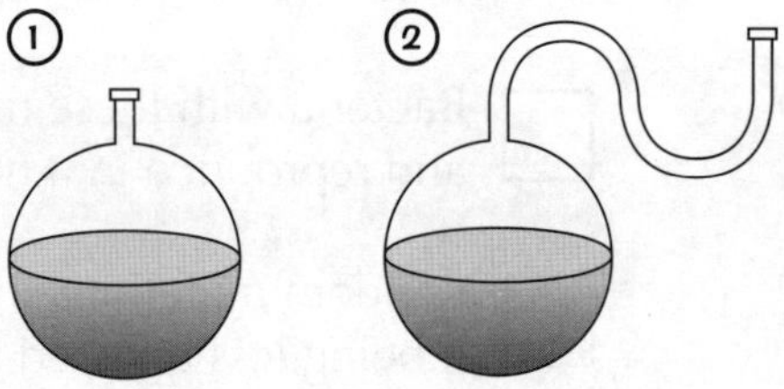

a) In which flask did the broth go bad, and why?

....

b) Explain why the broth in the other flask did not go bad.

....

c) In Pasteur's experiment, what is the purpose of Flask 1?

....

d) Suggest why Pasteur used a long curved neck for Flask 2, instead of sealing it with a stopper.

....

Yeast

Q1 a) Fill in the gaps to complete the symbol equation for anaerobic respiration in yeast.

$$C_6 \ldots\ldots_{12} \ldots\ldots_6 \rightarrow 2 \ldots\ldots{}_2H_5OH + \ldots\ldots CO_2 \text{ (+ energy)}$$

b) Write out the **word equation** for this reaction in the space below.

....

c) Complete the following sentences by choosing the correct word from each pair.

> In the absence of **oxygen / water**, yeast cells will respire **aerobically / anaerobically**.
>
> This is known as **photosynthesis / fermentation**.
>
> When **oxygen / water** is present they will respire **aerobically / anaerobically**.

Q2 The **growth rate** of yeast varies depending on the **conditions**.

a) Look at each of the graphs below and then choose the correct labels for the horizontal axes from the list provided.

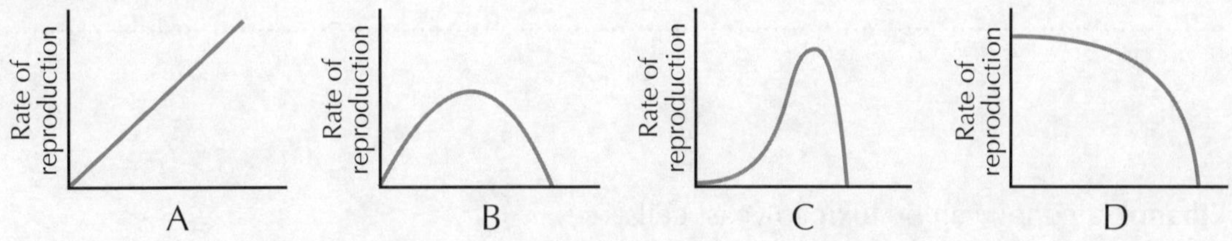

Temperature	Amount of food	Amount of toxic waste	pH

A .... **B** ....

C .... **D** ....

b) Suggest one way of measuring how fast a culture of yeast is reproducing.

....

Q3 Some **food-processing factories** produce sugary waste that they need to get rid of.

a) Suggest why the waste water from these factories should not be dumped into rivers.

....

....

b) Explain why yeast can be used to treat the waste water before it is released.

....

Brewing

Q1 There are four main stages in making **beer**.

a) Number these stages from 1 to 4, where 1 is the first stage and 4 is the last.

- ☐ The beer is drawn off.
- ☐ Sugar is extracted from barley grains and hops are added.
- ☐ The beer is pasteurised.
- ☐ Yeast is added and the mixture is incubated.

b) Explain the purpose of adding yeast.

....

c) State **two** things that it's important to prevent from entering the fermentation vessels during fermentation.

....

d) Sometimes **clarifying agents** are added to the beer at the end of the brewing process. What effect do clarifying agents have on the beer?

....

Q2 **Ethanol** (alcohol) can be **toxic** to yeast cells.

Complete the following passage using the words from the boxes below.

decreases | increases | anaerobically | high | tolerate | kill

Some words can be used more than once.

As yeast cells respire ...., the concentration of ethanol in the fermentation mixture .... This eventually starts to .... the yeast cells. As the cells begin to die, the rate of fermentation .... Different species of yeast are able to .... different concentrations of ethanol. The species that can survive in .... ethanol concentrations can be used to produce strong wine and beer with a .... alcohol content.

Brewing

Q3 Give the meanings of the following words connected with **brewing**:

a) Fermentation ....

b) Distillation ....

c) Pasteurisation ....

Q4 The method used to make **wine** is similar to that used to brew beer.

a) Describe fully the process used to produce wine.

....

....

....

b) Beer is often pasteurised at the end of the brewing process, but wine is not.
Explain this difference.

....

....

....

Q5 **Distillation** can increase the alcohol content of fermented liquids.

a) Explain how this process happens.

....

....

....

b) Distillation is a commercial process. Where must it be carried out?

....

Top Tips: Beer and wine have been made for yonks — long before people understood that they were using the process of **anaerobic respiration** to turn sugars into alcohol. Not that they cared.

Biofuels

Q1 Complete the following passage about biomass using the words from the boxes below.

transformed **organic** **biogas** **bacteria** **fermented** **wood** **energy**

Biomass is .... material. The ....
stored in biomass can be .... into more useful forms in
different ways. For example, ... from fast growing trees
can be burnt as a fuel, releasing heat energy. Dead organic material can be
.... by yeast or .... This process
generates ...., which can also be burnt as a fuel.

Q2 **Biogas** is produced by certain kinds of **microorganisms** when they decompose waste matter.

a) Name the **two** gases that are the main components of biogas.

....

b) Name **three** other gases that are found in biogas in smaller amounts.

....

c) What can be the danger of using biogas that contains around 10% methane?

....

Q3 Biogas is used as **fuel**. Draw lines to match how the fuel is used, to what it powers or produces.

Biogas is burned to heat water	Generates electricity
Burned to drive an engine	Produces steam to heat central heating systems
Burned to power a turbine	Powers cars and buses

Biofuels

Q4 **Bacteria** are used to produce **methane**, a component of biogas.

a) Describe how several different types of bacteria are used in the production of biogas.

b) Describe how methane can be produced on a large scale.

Q5 An experiment was carried out to investigate the effect of **different temperatures** on **biogas production** in four digesters. The table below shows the results of these investigations.

TEMPERATURE	BIOGAS PRODUCTION (litres/hour)
15 °C	0.2
25 °C	3.1
35 °C	9.2
45 °C	0.0

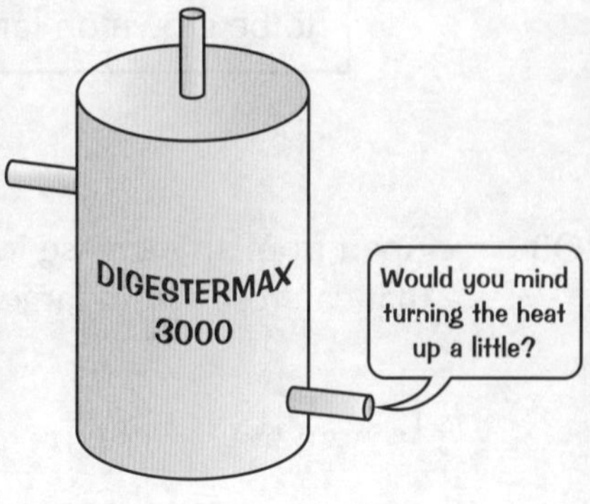

a) What was the best temperature for the production of biogas?

b) Suggest why more biogas was produced at this temperature than at any other temperature.

c) Suggest why biogas was **not** produced at 45 °C.

Top Tips: There's a lot to learn about biofuels — which is why there are a few more questions about them on the next page. Make sure you get to grips with this lot before turning over.

More on Biofuels

Q1 a) Write whether the following statements are **true** or **false**.

i) Biofuels are fossil fuels. ....

ii) Burning biogas doesn't produce particulates. ....

iii) Biogas isn't as 'clean' a fuel as diesel or petrol. ....

iv) Biogas contains less energy than natural gas. ....

b) Write a correct version of each false sentence in the space below.

....

....

Q2 Complete the passage below by circling the correct word(s) from each pair.

It's possible for biofuels to be produced and burnt without causing an overall increase in greenhouse gas levels. For this to happen, biofuels need to be burnt at the same **rate / temperature** that the biomass is produced and the plants need to be grown on land that **has / hasn't** been cleared by burning other vegetation.

Q3 Apart from an increase in greenhouse gas levels, give two possible **environmental problems** that can result from large areas of land being cleared to produce **biofuels**.

1. ....

2. ....

Q4 **Gasohol** is another **alternative fuel** which is widely used in some parts of the world.

a) Describe the composition of gasohol.

....

b) Give one use of gasohol. ....

c) Name one country where gasohol is used on a large scale. ....

d) The use of gasohol is only **economically viable** in areas with **small oil reserves**.
What else does an area need to make the use of gasohol economically viable?

....

Soils

Q1 The diagrams below show the particles in three different soil types — **sand**, **clay** and **loam**.

a) Label each soil type in the spaces provided.

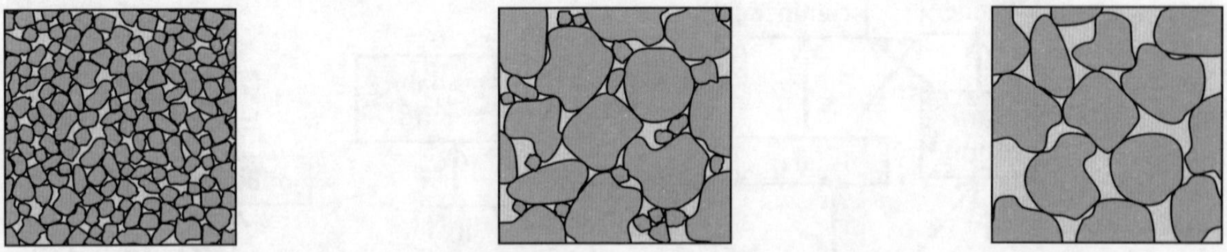

i) .... ii) .... iii) ....

b) **Clay soils** have a relatively low air content. Explain why this is in terms of **soil particle size**.

....

....

c) Most soils also contain **humus**. What is humus?

....

Q2 Darren has collected two samples of soil — one from his neighbour's vegetable patch, and one from his own vegetable patch. He wants to compare the **water content** of the two soil samples.

a) Describe how Darren might measure the water content of each soil sample.

....

....

....

....

b) The soil from Darren's vegetable patch is a sandy soil. His neighbour's soil is a clay soil. Which of these soils will have larger particles?

....

c) Explain how the particle size will affect the water content of the two soils.

....

....

Life in the Soil

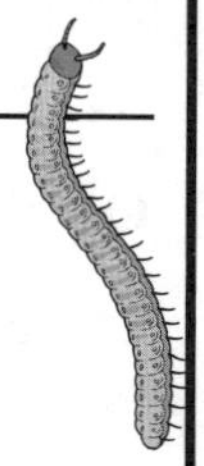

Q1 The diagram shows a food web from the soil in Nelson's garden.

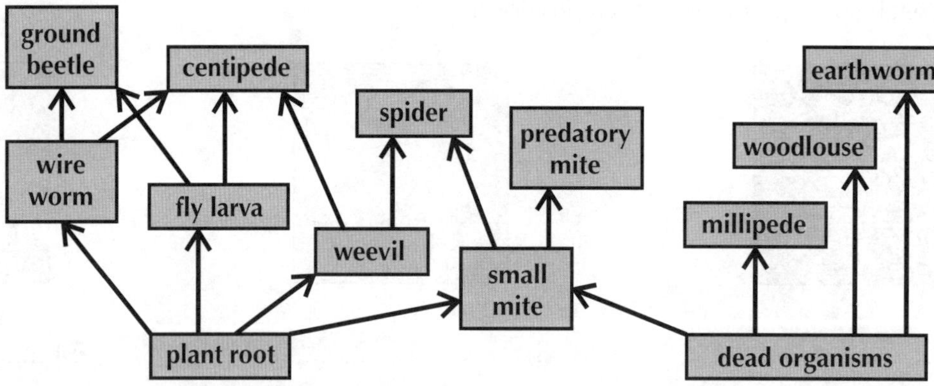

Nelson applied a pesticide to the soil which killed all the woodlice.
Explain how this may affect the following organisms:

a) Small mites ....

....

b) Wire worms ....

....

Q2 Explain why **humus** is important to life in the soil.

....

....

Q3 Complete the following passage about **earthworms**, using the words in the box below.

aeration	neutralise	Darwin	layers	nutrients	fertile	drainage	oxygen

Charles .... was one of the first people to discover why earthworms are so good for soil structure and fertility. One reason is that the worms' burrows allow air to enter the soil. This is called .... and it provides organisms in the soil with .... The burrows also increase ...., which prevents soil becoming waterlogged. Worm droppings help to .... soil acidity, making the soil more .... Their activities also help to mix up the soil ...., distributing .... more evenly.

Life in Water

Q1 Life in water and life on land are very different.
Give two **advantages** and two **disadvantages** of living in water.

....

....

....

Q2 Most species of crab, such as **spider crabs**, live in **water**. Other species, such as **robber crabs**, live on **land** and will actually drown if dropped into water.

Which species of crab — the spider crab or the robber crab — is likely to be more tolerant of changes in temperature? Give a reason for your answer.

....

....

Q3 Many **plants** that grow on land have **tough woody parts**.
Suggest why few plants found in **water** have woody parts.

Woody parts provide the plant with support.

....

Q4 The **Amoeba** is a single-celled organism that is found in **fresh water**. The solute concentration in an amoeba cell is **higher** than that of the surrounding water.

a) Suggest why the Amoeba tends to absorb too much water.

....

....

b) Explain the role of the contractile vacuole in preventing the Amoeba cells bursting.

....

....

c) Related species of single-celled organism living in the sea don't have a vacuole.
Suggest why not.

....

....

More on Life in Water

Q1 Nigel works for the **Environment Agency**. He's investigating reports that a **stream** (which runs alongside a farmer's land) has become covered in a thick blanket of **algae**.

a) What **substance** used in agriculture could be the cause of this algal growth?

....

b) **i)** Put the following sentences in order to describe the problems that rapid algal growth will cause.

- ☐ **Animals are unable to respire and die.**
- ☐ **Algae die and decay.**
- ☐ **Decomposers feed on dead algae.**
- ☐ **All the oxygen in the water is used up.**

ii) Name the **process** that causes rapid algal growth. ....

Q2 **Phytoplankton populations** can increase in ponds during the summer months.

a) Explain why phytoplankton populations usually increase in the summer and not the winter.

....

b) What effect will an increase in the phytoplankton population have on the zooplankton in the pond? Explain your answer.

....

Q3 State **three** possible **water pollutants**.

....

Q4 Complete the passage below about **photosynthesis in water** by filling in the missing words.

> Photosynthesis is affected by temperature, ... intensity and the availability of minerals. These factors change in different .... and at different depths. In winter and in deep water, light intensity and temperature are ...., so they limit the rate of photosynthesis. In the summer when .... and light intensity are ...., mineral concentration is much .... — so mineral concentration limits the amount of photosynthesis.

More on Life in Water

Q5 **Phytoplankton** are often the producers in ocean food webs.

a) Name another type of organism that often acts as a producer in **deep-sea** food webs.

....

b) Some deep-sea food webs rely on '**marine snow**' as a source of nutrients. What is 'marine snow'?

....

Q6 An investigation was carried out into the number of bacteria found along a stream. A **sewage outflow pipe** was located midway along the study site. The graph shows the number of bacteria found.

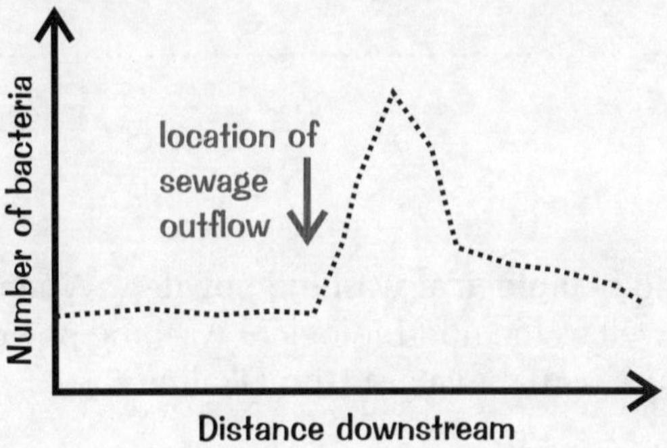

Explain the changes in levels of bacteria at increasing distance downstream from the outflow pipe.

....

....

Q7 **DDT** is a chemical that has been used as a **pesticide** to kill insects such as mosquitoes and lice.

a) Explain why DDT is passed along food chains.

....

....

b) Which organisms in a food chain are most likely to be poisoned by DDT? Explain your answer.

....

....

c) Name another chemical that can accumulate in food chains in the same way.

....

Enzymes in Action

Q1 **Biological washing powders** contain enzymes. One example is the **protease enzyme**.

a) Explain why protease enzymes are added to biological washing powders.

....

b) Name **two** other enzymes that can be added to biological washing powders and describe the function of each.

....

....

c) Explain why it is easier to remove stains once they have been digested by enzymes.

....

....

Q2 Andrea buys a new brand of **biological washing powder**. When she tries it out she finds it doesn't work as well as the non-biological washing powder she used to use. She decides this is because her tap water is **too alkaline**.

a) Explain why a biological washing powder might not work very well in alkaline tap water.

....

b) Andrea's dad thinks the washing powder would work better if she used a cooler wash cycle. Explain why biological washing powders work best at **moderate temperatures**.

....

Q3 Explain the role of the enzyme **invertase** in the **food industry**.

....

....

....

Top Tips: There are loads of different enzymes and we have loads of different uses for them — they've a role in everything from washing clothes to making food taste better. Remember though, all enzymes have a few things in common — and that includes being sensitive to temperature and pH.

More Enzymes in Action

Q1 Enzymes can be **immobilised** using various methods.

a) Describe how enzymes can be immobilised in **alginate beads**.

....

....

b) Circle two **advantages** of using immobilised enzymes from the list below.

Immobilised enzymes can be used in continuous flow processes.

Immobilised enzymes always work faster than normal enzymes.

Immobilised enzymes can be found naturally.

Immobilised enzymes don't contaminate the product.

Q2 Test strips used for detecting the presence of **glucose** in **blood** contain immobilised enzymes. When exposed to glucose in a blood sample, they cause a colour change at the tip of the strip. Suggest why **immobilised** enzymes are used.

....

....

Q3 Some people are **lactose intolerant**. They can only eat **dairy products** that have been treated to remove the **lactose** (milk sugar).

a) Explain why lactose intolerant people can't eat dairy products that contain lactose.

....

b) Describe what would happen if a lactose intolerant person drank milk containing lactose.

....

c) Describe how **immobilised enzymes** are used to produce lactose-free milk.

....

....

....

More on Genetic Engineering

Q1 What is a **transgenic organism**? Circle the correct definition from the options below.

A genetically modified organism

An organism that can't reproduce

An organism that reproduces asexually

A physically modified organism

Q2 Explain how it's possible for genes from one organism to function in another organism.

Q3 Bacteria can be genetically engineered to produce **human insulin**. Complete the passage below by circling the correct word(s) from each pair to explain how this is done.

> First, scientists must identify the gene that controls insulin production in humans. The gene is cut from the DNA with **restriction** / **ligase** enzymes, leaving **sticky** / **blunt** ends. A bacterial **plasmid** / **cell** is then cut open using the same enzymes. **Restriction** / **ligase** enzymes are used to join the ends of the insulin gene and the bacterial DNA together. The plasmid now contains the insulin **molecule** / **gene** and is taken up by bacteria. The bacteria reproduce rapidly, quickly resulting in millions of cells that can produce **ligase** / **human insulin**.

Q4 Plasmids are often used as **vectors** in genetic engineering. Explain what is meant by the term 'vector'.

Q5 Describe the role of **assaying techniques** in genetic engineering.

DNA Fingerprinting

Q1 Circle the correct word(s) to complete each of the following sentences about DNA fingerprinting.

a) Before DNA fingerprinting can start, the DNA must be **extracted / replicated.**

b) The DNA sample is broken down into fragments using restriction **acids / enzymes.**

c) DNA fragments are separated using **electric current / photographic film.**

d) Larger DNA fragments **move further than / don't move as far as** smaller DNA fragments.

e) DNA will show up on photographic film if it's been marked by a **radioactive probe / chemical stain.**

Q2 Choose from the words below to complete the passage about the **DNA fingerprinting** process.

positive **negatively** **bigger** **electrophoresis**
smaller **positively** **suspended** **negative** **separated**

After the DNA has been cut into fragments, these fragments are .... using a process called .... They're .... in a gel, and an electric current is passed through the gel. DNA is .... charged, so it moves towards the .... electrode (anode). .... bits travel faster than .... bits, so they move further through the gel.

Q3 The following **DNA samples** are being used in a **murder investigation**. The DNA samples are from the victim, three suspects and some blood which was found on the victim's shirt.

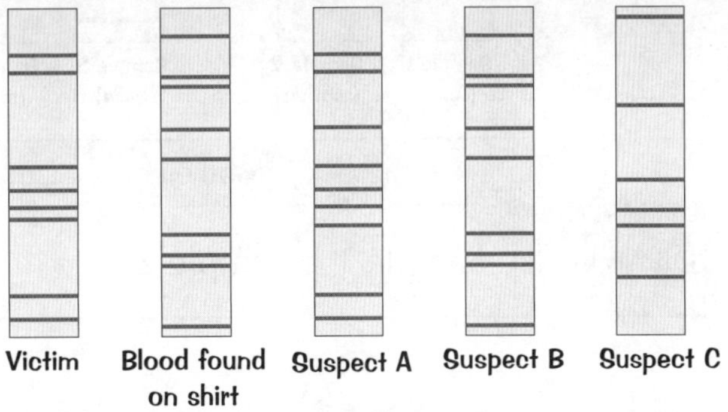

a) Which two individuals are likely to be **related** to each other? Explain your choice.

....

b) Who is the most likely culprit based on the DNA evidence? Explain your answer.

....

DNA Fingerprinting

Q4 Put the following stages of **DNA fingerprinting** into the correct order.

Compare the unique patterns of DNA.

Separate the sections of DNA.

Extract the DNA from the cells.

Cut the DNA into small sections.

1. ....

2. ....

3. ....

4. ....

Q5 A thoroughbred horse breeder has collected DNA samples from each of her horses. Her **new foal's DNA** is **sample 1**. The **mother** of the foal is **sample 2**. Study the **DNA profiles** and complete the table showing which horse is the **foal's father**.

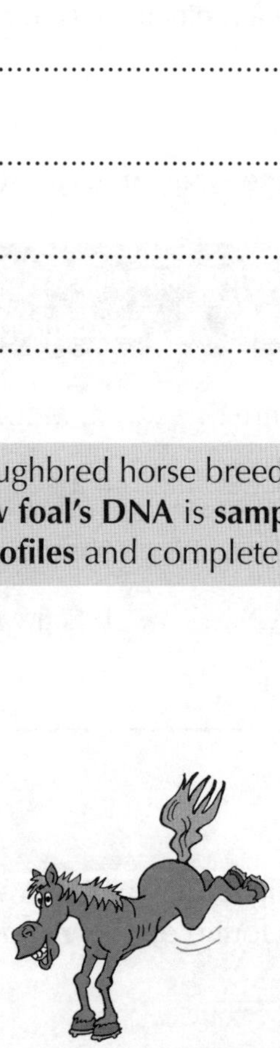

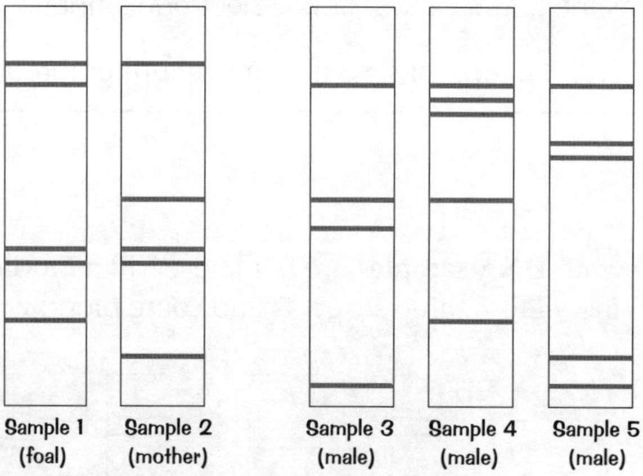

	Foal	Mother	Father
DNA sample	Sample 1	Sample 2	

Q6 A national **genetic database** would allow everyone's unique pattern of DNA to be saved on file.

a) Give one use of a national genetic database.

....

b) Give one drawback of a national genetic database.

....

Mixed Questions for Module B6

Q1 **Influenza** (flu) can be a fatal disease.

a) **i)** Name the type of microorganism that causes influenza.

....

ii) Describe the structure of this type of microorganism.

....

b) Explain why doctors shouldn't prescribe antibiotics to treat influenza.

....

Q2 The quality of the crops farmers grow is affected by the soil in their fields.

a) Why are earthworms beneficial to farmers with acidic soils?

....

b) Farmers often use fertilisers to improve the quality of their soil. Unfortunately, these fertilisers can cause eutrophication if they get into waterways. In the box below draw a flow diagram showing how fertilisers getting into water can lead to fish dying.

Q3 Some scientists are studying a species of shrimp that is very sensitive to **pH**. The shrimp is found in lakes with a pH **above 7.0**.

a) Name **one** other property of water that can be monitored by indicator species.

....

b) Describe how the scientists could use the shrimp as an **indicator species** for pH in other lakes.

....

....

Mixed Questions for Module B6

Q4 The rate at which **yeast** reproduces can be changed by controlling the conditions in which the yeast is growing.

a) Complete the following statements by circling the correct word from each pair.

i) Yeast reproduces **faster** / **slower** when oxygen is present.

ii) Yeast reproduces **faster** / **slower** with increasing temperature, until the **minimum** / **optimum** is reached.

iii) Before the **minimum** / **optimum** is reached, growth rate roughly **doubles** / **trebles** for every 10 °C rise in temperature.

b) Does yeast respire aerobically or anaerobically in the production of beer?

....

c) Write a balanced equation for the respiration of yeast in beer production.

....

Q5 a) Fill in the missing labels on the diagrams to show the main components of **biogas** and **gasohol**.

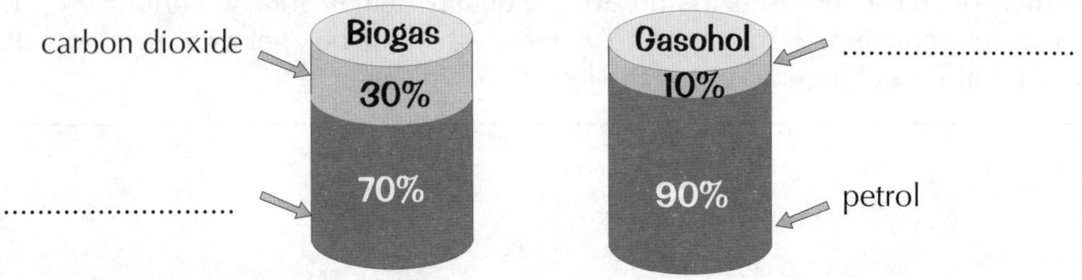

b) Suggest why it's important to monitor the level of the main component in **biogas**.

....

....

c) Give **three** uses of biogas.

....

d) Currently, most biogas is produced at around 35 °C. If the bacteria that produce the gas could be modified to produce biogas more efficiently at lower temperatures then biogas could be produced in cooler parts of the world.
Outline the stages that would be involved in modifying bacteria so that they respire more effectively at cooler temperatures if a suitable gene has been found in another organism.

....

....

....

Mixed Questions for Module B6

Q6 The soil in Zele's garden is described as a **loam soil**.

a) What is a 'loam soil'?

....

....

b) Zele is interested in the air content of his soil and decides to carry out an experiment to measure it. Describe an experiment that Zele could carry out to measure the air content of his soil.

....

....

....

....

c) **i)** The air content of a soil is important because many soil organisms depend on a good supply of **oxygen**. Explain why this is the case.

....

ii) Explain why soil organisms also depend on a supply of **water**.

....

Q7 Abigail studies food webs in the ocean.

a) Some of the food webs Abigail studies are **grazing food webs**. Explain what is meant by the term 'grazing food web'.

....

....

b) **i)** Suggest why **phytoplankton** are not found in deep-sea food webs.

....

ii) What type of organisms can act as producers in these deep-sea ecosystems?

....

c) Name **one** other source of nutrients in deep sea ecosystems.

....

Mixed Questions — Module B6

Q8 The diagram shows how bacteria can be **engineered** to produce **insulin**.

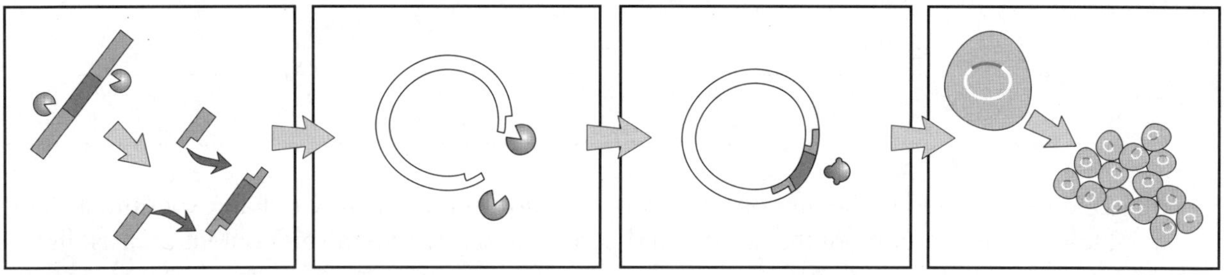

STAGE 1: The insulin gene is removed from the DNA of a human cell.

STAGE 2: A bacterial plasmid is cut open.

STAGE 3: The human insulin gene is inserted into the plasmid.

STAGE 4: The plasmid is taken up by bacteria — which are then cultured.

a) Where in a bacterial cell is a **plasmid** found?

....

b) In which stage(s) in the diagram are **ligase enzymes** used?

....

c) In which stage(s) in the diagram are **restriction enzymes** used?

....

d) In which stage(s) in the diagram are **assaying techniques** used?

....

e) The bacteria shown in stage 4 have been **genetically modified**.
What other name is often given to genetically modified organisms?

....

f) Explain why the human insulin gene will still work when transferred into the bacteria.

....

....

g) Bacteria can be **cultured** on an agar plate. Give **one** example of an **aseptic technique** that should be used when culturing bacteria in this way.

....

....